LIFE OF
LADY COLQUHOUN

by

JAMES HAMILTON, D.D., F.L.S.

PUBLICATIONS COMMITTEE
FREE PRESBYTERIAN CHURCH OF SCOTLAND
10 BEAUFORT ROAD, INVERNESS, U.K.

1969

Printed by
John G. Eccles, Henderson Road, Inverness

CONTENTS

FOREWORD

FROM its very inception the Gospel dispensation has accorded to noble women a place of prominence: and, while there was present a Peter, a John, a James, and others among the disciples of Jesus, there were also found among His immediate followers and acquaintances a Mary Magdalene, a Joanna, the sisters of Bethany, among others who, in their own station did worthily minister to the Saviour. In like fashion, at the time of these important events in the ecclesiastical history of Scotland which culminated in the Disruption of 1843, Christ's followers are inclusive of the names, not only of a Chalmers, Buchanan, Duncan, McCheyne and Burns, but also of one who was their female acquaintance, and who, in her own way, did not less truly serve the Redeemer — I refer to the worthy subject of this memoir, Lady Colquhoun of Luss.

Here we witness a remarkable and rare but not entirely unknown type of Christian. Herself a Sinclair of Thurso Castle and married to Colquhoun of Dumbartonshire, she occupied an unquestioned place among the ranks of the Scots nobility, but possession of higher *noblesse* — in respect of both title and spirit — as a daughter of Sion's King, becomes unmistakably apparent from Hamilton's biography and the autobiography of personal Journals so pleasingly conjoined in this book. Like the women of old time who trusted in God, Lady Colquhoun did, by Divine grace, adorn herself with incorruptible ornaments, and her great and varied usefulness in the Redeemer's vineyard derived its amazing strength from a life — although she confesses to its imperfections — of continual prayer and close communion with her Lord. "Go, and do thou likewise", is the constant challenge of these pages, as they also are interspersed with a great store of the *know-how* of practical godliness which the thoughtful reader will seek to turn to good account.

As a not inconsiderable writer to her own generation, Lady Colquhoun records her motive thus, "I feel a hope that the Lord will use me for His glory", and the same thought may suitably express the Committee's hope in sending forth the Life in a further edition.

ALEXANDER MURRAY, Convener.

Applecross, Scotland.
February 1969.

FOREWORD

WHEN the Editor was requested to compile this Memoir, he could not forget his scanty leisure, and his limited acquaintance with Lady Colquhoun. But the invitation of her family, the belief that a near relative of his own, now no more, would have responded to it with all the eagerness of his fervent nature, and the hope that such a narrative might be blessed to the reproduction of similar characters, at length induced him to make the attempt.

In the prosecution of his undertaking, the Compiler has felt both the lack and the excess of materials. To the affectionate diligence of a family who cannot revere too devotedly the memory of such a parent, and who have kindly put at his disposal all Remains and Recollections likely to illustrate her history, he is indebted for documents which might easily expand this memorial fourfold. On the other hand, many most valuable portions of her Ladyship's correspondence are gone beyond recall. One series of her letters perished in a conflagration; another was lost at sea; and many have disappeared as they passed into hands less careful than theirs who first received them. And, precious as is her Diary, having been kept for uses entirely personal, it contains few singular or extrinsic incidents. The difficulty of selection has been great. Many references are omitted which would have been peculiarly gratifying to relatives and friends: and many passages, in themselves so edifying, that their suppression caused a pang at the moment, and still leaves a misgiving. But, in a printed book, as in a public address, the writer well knows that the most venial fault is brevity; and his only grief will be, if, in trying to earn that pleasant censure, he has failed to do justice to one whose rare excellence merited a copious record and a more skilful biographer.

London, August 10, 1849.

CHAPTER I

O satisfy us early with Thy mercy; that we may rejoice and be glad all our days. — Psalm xc. 14.

> I do remember them, their pleasant brows
> So mark'd with pure affections, and the glance
> Of their mild eyes, when in the house of God,
> They gather'd up the manna that did fall
> Like dew around.
>
> Mrs Sigourney.

To few of her sons is Scotland more indebted than to the late Sir John Sinclair, of Ulbster. Entering into active life at an early age, for sixty busy years he was constantly spending in the service of his neighbours and his country excellent talents and a good estate. Whilst yet a lad at college he gave earnest of that passion for improvement, and that dauntless enterprise, which distinguished him through life. Among its many wants, his native Caithness wanted roads, and it was in vain that Mr Sinclair urged his brother landowners to supply the deficiency. There was a steep hill called Ben Cheilt, which ran right through the county, and as an objection to the turnpike, at once witty and fatal, it was always asked, "When will you show us a road over Ben Cheilt?" But one summer morning, having beforehand provided great store of implements, the young laird mustered on the spot 1,200 labourers, and ere nightfall a good carriage-way was thrown over this terrible mountain. And much of his subsequent career was the same exploit repeated. In every undertaking he knew that he must look for a Ben Cheilt — a Hill difficulty, on which all the timid and all the lazy would take their stand; and he always sought to surmount it by some brilliant and conclusive operation. And by dint of his own heroic exertions, and by the aid of those friends whom his reputation and his good offices were perpetually acquiring, he accomplished many works of enormous labor and of more than national utility. Encouraged by the success of his schemes for improving the husbandry of his own ungenial realms, he founded that Board of Agriculture which has introduced a new era in the tillage of the empire, whilst his untiring labors have left his name associated with the productive fisheries and thriving sheep-farms of Scotland. The list of his publications fills thirty pages of print; and if the themes be too various, and if fresh projects succeed one another too rapidly, they show the industry of the student who could impart information on subjects so diverse, and the benevolence of the statesman whose only concern was to make other people rich and contended. His "Statistical Account of Scotland"* is a trophy of his unconquerable energy and unwearied good-humour. It was a task for which, saving the engineer of Ben Cheilt, few would have had faith or preseverance sufficient. In order to compile it, he required answers to one hundred and sixty queries from nearly a thousand ministers. To many of his correspondents, such topics were strange or distasteful, and all of them encountered difficulties in the shyness, and sometimes in the superstition, of their natural informants. Tenants would not tell the produce of their farms for fear that their rents should be raised, and the Highland shepherds would not count their flocks, lest their vain curiosity

---

* In twenty-one volumes, octavo.

should entail a judgment on the fleecy people. But, by a judicious admixture of coaxing and objurgation, the sanguine Baronet quickened the diligence of the ministers, and by patience and adroitness, the ministers elicited the essential facts from their over-cautious parishioners. One laid aside his Cicero and another his "Poli Synopsis" till he should complete his census of pigs, poultry, and milch-kine. Professor Cooper grew archælogical over the "Auld Wives' Lift" and Dr Gibb waxed curious in acoustics:* in stately periods, worthy of a Scottish Johnson, Mr Sheriff told how many pounds of clover, and how many firlots of rye-grass were sown, in order to procure a hundred stones of hay; whilst the mellifluous cadence of Dr Mackinlay lent new charms to printed calicoes, duffles, serges, and mancoes, and all fabrics which owed their glory to Kilmarnock and to "creelman's com-position". When the mighty work was completed, no country possessed a survey of its internal resources so comprehensive, or local history so minute, as were con-tained in its elaborate pages. It greatly helped to create the science of statistics, and to the Scottish antiquarian it is a record of ever-growing value. When to such literary and economic toils, we add that in mellow age he could reckon two hundred of his countrymen who owed their worldly advancement to his friendly interposition, and that he numbered among his correspondents half the renowned names of Europe, we shall convey some idea of his wide acquaintance with his cotemporaries, as well

* Witness the clever and well-bred echo at Mugdock Castle; "Opposite to this tower is heard a very extraordinary echo. It repeats *any* sentence of six syllables, in the exact tone, and with the very accent, in which it is uttered; *waiting deliberately* till the sentence is finished before it begins." — *Stat. Acct.* xviii. 579.

as a specimen of his ceaseless and kind-hearted activity.*

When the heir of Ulbster was still young, full of the chivalry which through his strong-minded mother, Lady Janet,* he had derived from the ancient house of Sutherland, and exulting in all the possibilities of an existence which he meant to fill with noble deeds, at the residence of Mr Maitland, at Stoke Newington, he saw a young lady whose rare attractions drew many admirers round her. Of these none could be more ardent than Mr Sinclair, and he soon won the affections of a congenial mind. But Miss Maitland was an only child and an heiress, and her mother grudged that her future home should be so far away. However, the same love which would fain have kept her daughter near her, could not long gainsay that daughter's deliberate choice; and ere long the sanction of either parent gave to the happy suitor his lovely bride. Nine years passed prosperously. Mr Sinclair was in Parliament; his knowledge of finance made him an authority on that great question of the day, and gained him the special favour of the Premier. He had received the promise of a Baronetcy,* and was daily rising into

* For interesting memorials of Sir John Sinclair we are indebted to the filial affection of both a son and a daughter. See Miss Catherine Sinclair's "Shetland and the Shetlanders"; and "Memoirs of the late Right Honourable Sir John Sinclair, Bart.", by Archdeacon Sinclair.

* Lady Janet was daughter of William Lord Strathnaver, who, had he survived his father, would have been seventeenth Earl of Sutherland. Her sister, Lady Helen Sutherland, married Sir James Colquhoun, of Luss, grandfather of that Sir James who became the husband of Miss Janet Sinclair. Consequently, Lady Colquhoun and her husband were cousins.

* After his wife's death, as Mr Sinclair had no son, by a very unusual concession to the feelings of his friend, Mr Pitt made out the patent of Baronetcy in favour of Sir John, with remainder to his daughters and their heirs male.

higher political influence and public celebrity, when his flattering prospects were shrouded in sudden gloom by the removal of his much-loved partner. Along with the memory of her feminine graces and endearing gentleness, Mrs Sinclair left her representatives in two little girls, almost too young to miss her, but still so like her, that, in the daughters there was a promise that the mother would appear again. Hannah, the oldest, was five years of age, and Janet, of whom we are now to write, was only four. She was born in London, on the 17th of April, 1781, and during her infancy her parents resided at Westminster and Whitehall.

The first home of these motherless children was their ancestral seat, Thurso Castle. That stormy mansion looked more like a nursery for a lord of the isles, or like, what at first it was, the ocean-nest of the amphibious Caithness earls, than a retreat for tender orphans, cradled beneath a southern sun. But in that grim old castle the Orphans' Guardian had provided for them all but a mother's care. Not only was it the frequent resort of their fond surviving parent, but it was the permanent abode of their paternal grandmother, a Scottish gentlewoman of the olden school, shrewd, energetic, notable, proud of her ancient lineage, and, as became the descendant of that venerable peer who first affixed his tremulous autograph to Scotland's Covenant, a firm adherent to the Presbyterian polity; one who looked well to the ways of her household, and indited hortatory epistles to youthful clergymen; but also one who, amidst all the strictness of a manager, and all the stateliness of a high-born dame, carried about that constitutional kindliness, and those profound affections, which — like a deep well, fenced with rustic masonry — the old mothers of Scotland sometimes hid within a dry or stoic manner. Lady Janet now lived for the daughters of her son, and though perhaps imperfectly acquainted with the distinguishing truths of the Gospel, it was her anxiety to bring up her youthful charge religiously. She constantly took them to the parish church, and then examined them on the sermons they had heard, and required them every Sabbath to repeat to her a Psalm and the Shorter Catechism. At the Castle also resided their father's sister, a kind lady who, throughout her long life, never ceased to be much loved by her nieces.* And there, too, sojourned a judicious and affectionate servant — the English nurse, Morris — to whose warm-hearted counsels and simple Bible lessons her youthful charge were at that period more indebted than to any human influence. Herself a guileless and God-fearing Christian, this faithful attendant imbued their susceptible minds with much of her own truthfulness and reverence for sacred things. One Sabbath Miss Jessie came in with a lapful of shell-fish, which she had gathered on the shore at a great distance from the Castle. "I think, my dear," said Morris, "you should not have gathered them on the Sabbath-day; you had better put them again where you got them." Miss Jessie disappeared, and was late of returning. She had scrambled back the whole way along that rocky coast, till she came as nearly as she could judge to the spot where she had found the peri-winkles, and then put them carefully back again. To her latest day she retained the simplicity and ingenuousness, as well as the respect for the Sabbath, which she learned thus early; and to *her* latest day, Nurse Morris experienced the gratitude of the Misses Sinclair, who provided her with an ample annuity, and were careful that in health, as in sickness, she should want no comfort which money

---

* She afterwards became Mrs Baillie, by her marriage to Lord Polkemmet, one of the Senators of the College of Justice.

could procure.

From Thurso Castle it was a grand sight to view the
Pentland Firth in its winter's fury — and the sisters often
viewed it. On the short December days — in Caithness
extremely short — they would stand and watch as one
long wave after another swung home, and exploded
beneath them; till at last some monster billow, with
skirmishers streaming before him, rolled up to the charge,
and as he burst on the basement, the windows were
washed with brine, and the old tower shook like a light-
house. To gaze on that stormy ocean, and listen to its
noisy anthem, were great lessons; and even in these our
days of infant training, it might be well if more provision
were made for such bookless education, and the young
mind were permitted to commune more freely with nature
in her wild and gentle moods. The subject of this memoir
often reverted to the solemn and awe-struck emotions
with which she used to survey the many waves of that
mighty sea. To her it lived. In its gambols it was a
familiar and a play-fellow; in its turmoil it was a preacher
of Jehovah's majesty; and when formal instructions had
nearly faded from remembrance, she was still conscious
of lofty thoughts, and gave impressions, derived from
this august but kindly tutor.

From Thurso Castle Lady Janet brought her grand-
daughters to Edinburgh. There, for three years they
dwelt in the ancient Canongate, whose quaint houses
were still occupied by such of the aristocracy as had not
migrated to the New Town; and then, to complete their
education, they were sent to the school at Stoke Newington, where their own mother had spent her youthful days.
Mrs Crisp, by whom this school was conducted, received
the children of her former pupil with a very warm
affection, and, in her well-ordered establishment, the

business of learning went briskly forward. The different branches were taught by the best teachers; the Miss Sinclairs enjoyed good health, and were endowed with excellent abilities; they had already acquired the most essential elements of knowledge before coming to London, and they had every incentive to study which the affection of their governess and the goodwill of their companions could supply. Accordingly, they made signal proficiency, and when, at the respective ages of fifteen and sixteen, they returned to Edinburgh, in person and acquirements advanced beyond their years, they found a ready welcome into that brilliant society to which their birth was a passport, and into which their kind mother-in-law, Lady Sinclair,* rejoiced to introduce them.

However, it was the great happiness of the sisters that even then they had no love of fashion and no turn for gaiety. And it was their other great happiness that they had an ardent love for one another. Hannah was a student. Even during her childish days at Thurso, she had nearly as many friends as there were books in her father's library. She knew the haunt of each, and climbing on a chair got hold of her favourite poet or divine, and sat demurely reading whilst the summer tempted her to play. To her it was the great event, not when the carrier brought a package of new toys, but a parcel of new volumes; and when ministers and learned people visited the Castle, she posed them with hard questions. At school the same tendency bewrayed itself. Her turn was still for

---

* The second wife of Sir John Sinclair was the only daughter of Lord Macdonald. She was not more eminent for beauty and accomplishments, than for benevolence and sweetness of disposition. The attachment of the Misses Sinclair towards her was warm and well-deserved, for she was always a kind mother, and a faithful friend to them. She survived her husband ten years, and died in 1845.

thought and knowledge. She was fond of languages; she was an adept in grammar, history, geography, arithmetic; she could calculate an eclipse, or analyse "Reid's Inquiry". And, as might be expected, she was sedate and speculative, and often silent. From extreme modesty, reserved, she was still more self-contained, because amongst companions of her own sex she seldom found much sympathy in her intellectual pursuits. But Jessie was more lively. Dutiful and diligent, and considerate of each one's feelings, she was full of merry life and social glee. There was health in her nimble step and a prepossession in her fair and open features, and a peculiar charm in her tuneful voice. To her sister's turn for music she added a remarkable command of the pencil; and whilst her sister pored over problems and deep authors, Jessie read for information. Their characters had just diversity sufficient to increase their fondness for one another, and to enable the one to supply what the other lacked. For her erudite and thoughtful sister the younger felt an admiring and up-looking deference; whilst the limpid perceptions and true instincts of that younger mind often proved lights in dark places to the more abstract inquirer.

At that period Dr Walter Buchanan was one of the ministers of Canongate. His warm and affectionate nature had been cast in the mould of the Gospel, and as it shone from his happy countenance and breathed in his gracious words, holiness was very beautiful.* The sisters looked

* Dr Walter Buchanan was born in 1755. After he was licensed he received an invitation to become the pastor of the Scotch Church at Rotterdam, and was also called to the chapel of South Leith, of which Dr Colquhoun was for so many years the eminent minister. But instead of either charge he accepted the office of assistant to Mr Randall, of Stirling, whom he succeeded in 1780. In 1789 he was translated to the Collegiate Church and parish of Canongate, where he remained until his death in 1832. He was a beautiful specimen of Christian urbanity

at him with reverence. They had been told a great deal
about religion, and they thought of it as something strict
and precise; but they had never met anything so fascin-
ating as they saw in their saintly pastor. They were quite
arrested. Even amidst gay parties and volatile companions there followed them many a reminiscence of
those fervent intercessions and persuasive counsels to which
they had hearkened on the previous Sabbath. At last one
day Miss Sinclair said to her sister, "If to obtain eternal
life, we have only to practise goodness; if we have only
to do what is right in the sight of God and avoid what is
evil, I am sure it would be folly not to make the attempt."
And the proposal was made to one who had already been
pondering the matter in her own mind, and who was
beginning to be much impressed with the value of her
soul and the uncertainty of life. The two resolved to

and warm-heartedness, and his house was the natural resort of
the pious clergymen and Dissenters who in those days — the
days of Simeon, Rowland Hill, and George Burder — came to
Edinburgh, and who, until the year 1799, were allowed to occupy
indiscriminately the pulpits of the Scottish Establishment. Along
with Dr Davidson he was noted for his liberal encouragement of
pious students of Theology, and by the books which he lent them,
the fatherly advice which he gave them, and the many substantial
services which he rendered them — finding a tutorship for one,
and the office of schoolmaster or assistant minister for another,
and frequently giving goodly sums to those in straitened circumstances — he became a general patron to all probationers of
Evangelical sentiments in Edinburgh. For many years he edited
a periodical which supplied the godly families in Scotland with
missionary intelligence and instructive Sabbath-reading — "The
Religious Monitor". With that constancy which was one of her
loveliest characteristics, Lady Colquhoun never abated for one
hour in the grateful and venerating affection with which she regarded this earthly guide of her youth; and when, long afterwards, her own daughter was married, she felt it a hallowing
and auspicious circumstance that the rite was solemnized by her
own spiritual father. And in his widow, who survived for fifteen
years, she found one of her most esteemed and congenial friends.
The house of Mrs Buchanan was the last to which Lady C. paid
a visit.

become religious. They often retired and read the Bible together, and became very exact in devotional exercises. But still they were not satisfied. They saw that their pastor and Christians like him, "had bread to eat which they knew not of", and they longed for this hidden manna. At this time they found on their father's table a Theological Treatise, newly published and inscribed "From the Author". It was "A Practical View of the Religious System of Professed Christians in the Higher and Middle Classes, by William Wilberforce, M.P." It seemed the very book they wanted. They carried it off to their own apartments and perused it with avidity. They could easily recognise in it the same system of evangelical doctrine which their minister preached, and as one truth after another unfolded in the bland and eloquent expositions of the gifted author, they were transported with delight. In the precision of a printed book, and in the free, inartificial language of a layman, they understood the Gospel. In Christ believed they found their peace with God; in Christ loved they learned a new morality. It was Dr Buchanan's scriptural preaching and elevated walk which first prepossessed them in favour of vital godliness, and which long continued to be the chief means of building them up in faith and holiness; but it was the "Practical View" which first corrected their self-righteous errors and first taught them God's own method — the religion of receiving and relying.

After this the Canongate Church was dearer than ever. With sacred delight they hailed the return of the Sabbath, and to them the most hallowed spots in the world were the dusky pulpit in which re-appeared that man of God, and their own family pew with its faded lining of green baize. With its brown light, its heavy pillars, and clumsy sounding-board, and with an audience becoming rapidly more and more plebeian, that sanctuary had charms which more classical structures and more fashionable resorts could never countervail. It was the Bethel where God first met them, and during each sojourn in Edinburgh, the youngest sister used always to revisit it, till shortly before the time when she arrived at "her Father's house in peace".

Now, also, was found the benefit of "two walking together". Miss Sinclair's seriousness and reflectiveness at an earlier period had proved of essential service to Miss Janet; and now that service was requited, for, indulging the metaphysical propensity of her mind, Miss Sinclair was soon involved in perplexity as to the primary truths of revelation.* The doctrines of the Trinity, the incarnation, the eternity of future punishment, the Divine sovereignty, all in succession proved stumbling-blocks; and though much distressed at her own reluctant doubts, she had not within her own resources the means of removing them. In spiritual matters her only confidant was her youngest sister; but a mind like hers could not have sought a better counsellor. To Miss Janet the Gospel had always been its own witness. She did not "exercise herself in great matters"; but she saw the glory of God in the face of Jesus Christ. To her the religion of the Bible was beautiful. To her, in His revealed character, God was light, and she perceived no darkness at all. To her the Bible was truth, and the Gospel was the wisdom of God. And instead of debating with her sister, she directed her mind to the same objects which had assured herself. That which she had seen of the Word of Life she declared to her disquieted friend; and by dwelling

---

* We here anticipate the narrative by a few years. It was not till Miss S. had reached her 21st year that she felt the doubts described above.

on the fitness of the Gospel, and the loveliness of the Saviour's character, and by urging her to pray, she sought to bring that friend to "fellowship with the Father, and with his Son Jesus Christ". And she succeeded. By means of the more prominent and practical truths of Christianity, she conjured away her sister's abstruser doubts and intellectual difficulties, and had the happiness to see that dearest of her kindred a sharer of her own ingenuous and healthful piety. Our language contains few summaries of Evangelical Christianity more simple and comprehensive than Hannah Sinclair's "Letter on the Principles of the Christian Faith"; and in reading it we feel our interest deepened by remembering that this labor of sisterly love is in good measure the result of sisterly prudence and piety; for, under the blessing of God the Spirit, it was her younger sister's meekness of wisdom and simplicity in Christ which mainly contributed to establish Hannah Sinclair in the "Christian Faith".

But an event had now occurred which, whilst it left them attached as ever, interrupted their daily communings. On the 13th of June, 1799, and in the nineteenth year of her age, Miss Janet Sinclair was united in marriage to James, eldest son of Sir James Colquhoun of Luss, Baronet.

CHAPTER II

Grow in grace, and in the knowledge of our Lord and Saviour
Jesus Christ. — 2 Peter iii. 18.

> Lady, that in the prime of earliest youth
> Wisely hast shunn'd the broad way and the green,
> And with those few art eminently seen,
> That labour up the hill of heavenly truth,
> The better part, with Mary and with Ruth,
> Chosen thou hast.
> Thy care is fixed, and zealously attends
> To fill thy odorous lamp with deeds of light,
> And hope that reaps not shame.
>
> Milton's Sonnets.

HAS the reader ever spent a bright day on Loch Lomond?
Has he gone at leisure, and carried to it a spirit free
from guilt and foreboding? Rising in health and in
prayer, has he opened his soul and consented beforehand
to let in all the wonder and delight with which the great
Creator may be pleased to fill it? And, in his own hired
boat, dropping from isle to isle, has he taken time to
gaze and meditate and dissolve into the scene? And was
there ever day like that? Not that you can describe the
sights unutterable; though you carry within yourself
placid visions and sunny images of which you know that
the origin was there : a silvery fulness, and, standing
forth from it, mossy rocks and clumps of verdure; a
giant mountain on a throne of empyrean, with a foot-
stool of lazulite; vistas through the hot and flickering

air, such as the fire-tinted pencil of Turner only can
depict; pure summits and a polished flood, which made
you think of the hills of immortality, and the snowy robes
which sweep the sea of glass : whilst, like the music
which breaks a dream and then makes it beatific, through
all the trance there went and came the sense of a pervading Presence — the nearness of that Eternal Wisdom
which built the mountain and up to its green edging
brimmed the flood. But though no words can restore the
landscape, you remember how it refined your perception
and ennobled all your faculties : the fallow-deer on Inch-
lonaig and Inchmurrain grew tall as the elk, and you
were sure that the hawk was an eagle. The *Persicaria* in
the bays, with its rosy spikes, and the toad-flax on the
beach, were new and gorgeous flowers; and familiar texts
and stanzas of favourite hymns thrilled you with excessive
emotion. You had put off the commonplace, and were
clothed upon with fine and pellucid senses; and there was
no longer aught tame or vulgar in the world, for you
yourself were nobler.

With a keen eye for its varied beauties, the subject of
our biography now found her home in one of the loveliest
regions of all these lovely shores. Surrounded by its stately
trees, and sheltered from the blast by the ferny slopes of
a Highland mountain, Rossdhu looks out upon Loch
Lomond, where its waters are widest and its isles and
margins fairest.* And, though encompassed by soft lawns

* A small volume has been compiled, describing the sensations
of different travellers in visiting Niagara. A similar volume
might be devoted to Loch Lomond. Such experiences are interesting. Be it the perfection of grandeur or the perfection of beauty,
the tendency of noble scenery is to concentrate the soul, and
nothing can be more revealing of the real character than the
genuine utterance of such intensified moments. And, after the
lake in all its loveliness had subsided into her calm and daily
consciousness, few things were more delightful to Lady Colquhoun

and blossoming parterres, it is near enough to the mountains to be constantly visited by breezes from the broom and the heather. Some of the windows look out on a ruined gable of that castle from which the fierce Sir Humphrey used to sally with his followers when he went to fight the Clan Gregor; and near that castle, overshaded by ancient yews, is the roofless chapel, where the fierce Sir Humphrey was laid to sleep when all his fights were over. With its pictures and its library and its spacious halls, with three parishes for its manor and the queen of Scottish lakes for its outlook, and with all the self-contained luxury which marks the country-seat of a wealthy Baronet, at the period of life most susceptible of enjoyment, the younger Miss Sinclair found herself

than to witness the rapture of a fervent novice. Near the mansion of Rossdhu is the Island of Inchtavanach, from whose elevated crest, tradition says, a great bell used to summon to their several churches the people of four parishes. Of course, this belfry-knoll commands a splendid view; but, owing to his lameness, it was with some difficulty that they dragged Legh Richmond to the summit. Once there, however, they could not drag him down; but, slowly revolving his radiant visage, and through his great round-eyed spectacles devouring the landscape, he always hushed his fidgetty companions with the sentence — "The eye is not satisfied with seeing." But a shorter glance sufficed his friend and cotemporary, Mr Simeon, of Cambridge. With his usual vivacity he pirouetted round to look at every object as they pointed it out; then, turning to his hospitable guide, he exclaimed, "Sir James, you turn to this side and you say, 'That is mine'; and you turn to the other side and say, 'That is mine'; but," lifting both his hands, "I look up and say, Heaven is mine!" On the same spot Dr Chalmers exclaimed, "I wonder if there will be a Loch Lomond in heaven!" And there Dr Malan knelt down, and poured forth the fulness of his heart in such a prayer as many have heard beside his own Lake of Geneva. Perhaps, however, the mood of mind most congenial to her own was that expressed by one whom she never personally knew. In the diary lately published of the devoted missionary, John Macdonald, he writes— "I took an opportunity of visiting Loch Lomond, and was exceedingly delighted. O how sweet and tranquil was the bosom of the lake! I thought of the 'peace of God that passeth understanding'."

the lady of Rossdhu.* But the grace of God had full possession of her mind, and, amidst all the blandishments of smooth-going existence, He Himself was her chiefest joy, and His Word her chosen guide. Amidst all the charms of the landscape and all the fascinations of refined society, she never neglected a household duty. "The lines have fallen to me in pleasant places," was her devout acknowledgment regarding her earthly lot; and, though embowered in scenes so fair that they almost justified the relaxation to which they perpetually tempted, she never ceased to hear a voice, authoritative and earnest, saying, "Occupy till I come."

Of retiring habits, and fain to dwell among his own people, Sir James Colquhoun was much beloved by his dependants. Personally cognizant of their character and circumstances, there survived betwixt himself, his farmers, and cotters, the best relic of feudalism — its mutual affection. He took the principal management of his own estates, and never turned adrift on the world the orphan or the widow.* It was his greatest happiness to have a wife like Lady Colquhoun. At first, proud of her looks and her elegant manners, he learned to value her gentle wisdom and unworldly goodness, till at last harmony of affection merged in harmony of faith. She saw his prejudices against evangelical religion. She scarcely hoped to remove them by conversation; but she prayed for

* Her father-in-law died, and she became Lady Colquhoun, in 1805.

* In early life Sir James had served in the army. Having raised a company in his own neighbourhood, according to the regulation at that period, he was appointed to the command of it, and thus joined his Regiment with the rank of Captain. He was afterwards elected Member of Parliament for the county of Dumbarton. On the death of his father he retired from the army, and chiefly resided on his estate, devoting himself to its improvement.

"oil in her lamp", and sought to make her own light shine. Her prayers were answered; her consistency was rewarded. Her husband became gradually and more and more intelligently attached to the same principles. In appointing pastors to the eight parishes of which he was patron, it was his first anxiety to find ministers of fervent piety. And when, by and by, he was chosen an elder of the Church, and had a voice in its supreme Assembly, his vote was always given for those measures which conferred privileges on Christian congregations, and which promised most effectually to extend the Gospel.

Luss can boast of more than one celebrated divine. It was here that Maclaurin commenced his eminent ministry, and here that he would have been content to spend his life in preaching those sermons so full of holy eloquence and magnificent theology. And it was here that John Colquhoun was born. In his boyhood he herded sheep on the Mulea Hill, and till thirty years of age plied the shuttle of a hand-loom weaver, when he got his heart's desire — went to College, and became one of the most useful preachers and solid authors of the Scottish Church. But, for many years after Lady Colquhoun came to Rossdhu, the parish minister was Dr John Stuart. Although not eminent as a preacher, he was famed for his scholarship and his scientific attainments. To his knowledge of the original Scriptures, and to the idiomatic purity of his Gaelic, the Highlanders are mainly indebted for the perfection which their version of the Bible has attained. And at a time when few cared for natural history, he was pursuing it with enthusiasm among the mountains of Breadalbane; and with such success, that when Pennant, Lightfoot, and Sir Joseph Banks came to explore the Scottish Fauna and Flora, it was from Mr Stuart they derived their most important information.

The "Manse Garden", at Luss, contained many exotic rarities, and, still more interesting to the botanist, many of the scarcest plants of Scotland; and in that garden it was a great delight to Lady Colquhoun to walk, and view those treasures with which no hand might tamper save the Doctor's own. In these visits she was soon much prepossessed in favour of the minister's eldest daughter. Along with her father's warmth and generosity, Miss Stuart inherited much of his talent and his turn for botany. She was often the companion of his rambles through the glens and up the mountains, and, having on these occasions shared all the delight of his discoveries, she could guide the curious traveller to the spot where *Lysimachia thyrsiflora* or the *Osmunda regalis* flourished, and knew where on Ben Lomond might be gathered the finest specimens of the *Sibbaldia procumbens* and the purple Saxifrage. But, in that amiable and ardent mind, Lady Colquhoun quickly recognised an affinity more precious still. Miss Stuart's thoughts were deeply occupied with those great truths in which she herself had found all her salvation and all her desire; and, until Miss Stuart's marriage to an eminent minister, when they met they took every opportunity to commune together on the things which pertained to their everlasting peace. In one of these walks round the garden at the manse Lady Colquhoun stopped to admire a beautiful dwarf-shrub (the *Rhododendron ferrugineum*). Next morning, on entering the breakfast-room, she found a tiny slip of the plant in a miniature flower-pot; it grew, and soon needed a larger receptacle, and ere long was transferred to a choice plat of the flower-garden; and, on her return from any temporary absence, one of the first spots which Lady Colquhoun was sure to visit was this border, that she might see "dear Betsy Stuart's plant". The place no longer knows either, but the memorial of their hallowed affection, the little shrub, with its clusters of rich crimson, still flourishes.

However, during the first years of her married life, Lady Colquhoun had much reason to lament the want of Christian society. Her spirit craved for it. All her desire was towards the excellent of the earth, and when, with letters of introduction, pious strangers took their place at her table, or turned aside to tarry for a night, she had towards them a venerating feeling, as if they were angels of God. But usually it was in vain that she longed to have spiritual conversation with them. They assumed that she was like most gentlewomen of that day — more amiable and interesting than many, but as destitute of real religion as the rest. And then, when they had passed on their way, and when it would have been equally just to have charged the lost opportunity to their excessive prudence or erroneous politeness, her sensitive spirit took home all the blame, and she upbraided herself for her sinful timidity. On the other hand, in the visiting circle of her own neighbourhood there were at that time few, at least few known to her, in whose intercourse she could find spiritual invigoration or intellectual enjoyment. Amongst the landed aristocracy of Scotland there were then less mental expansion and less religious enlightenment than in the middling class of towns-people, and much less than amongst their own modern representatives. Political rancour was extremely virulent. The prejudice against evangelical Christianity was nearly universal. And if the gentlemen did not drink so freely nor swear so coarsely as a bygone generation, they did not read their Bibles more, nor keep the Sabbath better. Card-parties, elaborate carriage airings, and the news of the neighbourhood, were the recreations of their wives and daughters;

but few took pains to cultivate their minds, and still fewer were engaged in works of usefulness; so that in the general absence of literary tastes and refined enjoyments, the houses of our Scotch grandees repeated with awful uniformity the same scenes of pompous inanity and stolid merry-making. And, although there were exceptions, all the more prized for their rarity, it was rather by an effort of benevolence than in obedience to her natural inclinations that the young lady of the manor paid visits which added nothing to her mental resources, and often left repentant misgivings in her devout and conscientious mind.

This comparative isolation was not without its benefits. It gave a more personal character to her piety. Instead of deriving all her impressions and impulses from ardent or endearing friends, her religion increasingly became communion with the Saviour. And it left her more leisure for that employment into which she had thrown all her soul — the instruction and training of her children. And, whilst it prepared her for hailing with peculiar delight the congenial intercourse at length so abundantly vouchsafed to her, it drew her in the meanwhile with especial tenderness towards such humble disciples as the parish then contained — those "poor" whom the Lord had promised that she should "have always".

Judging by the hand-writing, it was soon after her arrival at Rossdhu that the following "Helps to Self-Examination" were written out :—

" HELPS TO SELF-EXAMINATION.

" 1. Did I awake as with God this morning?

" 2. How were the secret devotions of the morning performed?

" 3. Did I offer my praises of thanksgiving, and renew the dedication of myself to God with becoming attention and affections?

" 4. How did I read the Scripture or any other useful book? Did they do my heart good?

" 5. How have the mid-day devotions been attended to?

" 6. Have I pursued my common business with diligence as unto the Lord?

" 7. What time have I lost this day, and for what cause?

" 8. Have I seen the hand of God even in little mercies and afflictions?

" 9. Have I received my comforts with thankfulness and my afflictions with resignation?

" 10. How have I guarded against passion and vanity?

" 11. Have I lived by the faith of the Son of God?

" 12. Have I governed my thoughts well, especially in solitude?

" 13. What subject of thought was chosen this day, and how was it regarded?

" 14. Has my heart this day been full of love to God and to all mankind?

" 15. How have I profited this day by the negligences I observed in last night's examination?

" 16. How did I pray last night? "

In the hope that it might prove a stimulus to increased activity, and a help in the great business of self-culture, in 1805 she began to keep a Diary. Its precious volumes have been intrusted to the perusal of the Editor, and have left on his mind a very sacred impression regarding the sainted writer. And although extracts will probably fail to transfer that impression in its fulness to the mind of the reader, they may give him some idea of the tender lowlihood, the faithful self-observation, the ingenuous truthfulness, the simple dependence, and the devout aspirations, which resulted in a character at last so complete and blameless. As illustrative of her calm and constant nature it may be right to notice how perseveringly this private narrative was kept up. Perhaps the reader has himself tried to keep a journal. In a zealous moment he has commenced a daily register of employments, or the story of a tour, or a record of his experiences; but he soon wearied of its methodical routine, and the written leaves have long since been cut away to render the book available for some new project. But Lady Colquhoun was eminently stedfast. Her undertakings were never prompted by romantic fancies, but by sober judgment; and, therefore, the longer she persisted in them the more she liked them. And the successive volumes of this journal, extending over forty years, and sustained with scarcely an interruption, are only a symbol of that continuous industry with which she prosecuted every enterprise, and that loving faithfulness with which she clung to all her friends.

During the first period this Diary is usually brief; but a few specimens may throw some light on the writer's position and employments :—

"*Tuesday, Oct. 15*, 1805—Awoke in an unhappy frame; but was enabled to pray with fervour. Prayed for an unlikely thing, which I hoped might be helpful to my spiritual interests. To my astonishment my prayer was heard. Called at Cameron. Mr Slight came to dinner. Much benefited by his prayer."

Mr Slight was then, and for a few years longer, the Minister of Bonhill. He was a man of cultivated mind and fervent piety. He sometimes, but not often, spent a day at Rossdhu, and "the unlikely thing" for which Lady Colquhoun had prayed on the above occasion was, that he might be sent to their house that day. In going to Cameron she met Mr Slight, who stopped his horse, and said that he was on his way to Rossdhu, and if convenient to her, he would still proceed. The Journal resumes:—

"*Wednesday, 16.* — Arose with God. Mr Slight left us. The joy of God's salvation restored. I would do anything for a continuance and increase of it. Retired twice to read and pray for some time during the forenoon.

"*Saturday, Dec. 28.* — Resolved to read no more novels, having been enticed to read one which too much occupied my time. Retired and read and prayed with much love and trust in my Lord. This week and last I have seen how unable I am to resist temptation. Oh! that Christ would strengthen me !

"*Saturday, July 21,* 1810. — Prayed earnestly to be kept from worldly-mindedness this day, being to dine at ———. Escaped pretty well at the dinner-party; but I fear transgressed in the evening at the theatre, where I went without wishing it."

As, in the sequel of this Journal, there will be no allusion to the theatre, it may be right to mention, that up to this period, and in deference to the wishes of others, Lady Colquhoun occasionally went to it; but she had long ceased to feel happy there. With successive visits her repugnance strengthened, and soon after the above was written she saw so clearly the sinfulness of patronising such places, that she made a decided stand, and never entered a playhouse again.

"*Sunday, Aug. 12.* — Do not remember for a long time being so little disposed for the services of the day. Prayed in the morning seriously, but with little life. Unfortunately no service at Luss.* Read a sermon aloud, but felt little

* The communion was then dispensed in most rural parishes only once a year; and, as the pastors and flocks of adjacent

interested. Heard the children, and by reading Doddridge's
'Rise and Progress' tried to find out what I should do
when this deadness is upon me. Read over this book and
felt a little enlivened by finding some of my own experience in it. In temptation without Christ I cannot
conquer; but through Him I may surely do all things.
Let me struggle on in the way of duty; He cannot forsake
his own servants. Lord, Lord, help! — After writing the
above, retired to pray to my Lord. Entreated with great
fervour to be supported in the ways of God, in the midst
of innumerable evils. In prayer my faith and love revived.
How gracious is my Lord!

"*Thursday, 23.*— Delighted with some pleasing accounts
of George.

"*Friday, Oct. 12.* — Sir J. and Lady M'Gregor Murray
here. Read and prayed early.

"*Saturday, Oct. 13.* — This whole day so engaged as
to find it impossible to read the Bible. Prayed in the
forenoon, and felt affected while walking in the island
among the tombs.*

"*Sunday, Nov. 25.* — Read, with delight, 'Theron and
Aspasio', on the freeness with which Christ is offered.
Retired and prayed, with tears, for acceptance and
pardon.

"*Sunday, April 14*, 1811. — Have been three months in
Edinburgh, from which I returned about a week ago;
and though constant occupations of one sort or other
have prevented my writing, I now set my hand to it that
God is true and merciful to those who trust in Him. I

parishes used to adjourn to the scene of its celebration, each
pulpit was apt to be vacant several times in the course of the
summer.

* Inch Cailliach is the burying-place of the M'Gregors.

left this place fearful that the dissipations of an Edinburgh winter would draw my thoughts from my only real good; but, merciful Lord, thou hast made me more than conqueror! My prayer was, that thou wouldest shine as a light around me in temptation, and surely thou hast heard me. The means of grace were powerful, and by the Holy Spirit working in them, far outdid any contrary influence. The Sabbaths I was able regularly and delightfully to keep, and I had an opportunity of sitting down at the table of the Lord when Dr Buchanan preached — a time which I hope was not lost to me. Now I return here to the want of those lively means; but, Lord, thou art here also. Hold thou me up, and I shall be safe; and so shall I keep thy statutes continually.

"*Wednesday, April 17.* — Prayed fervently in the morning. Resisted a temptation to anger. This day I am thirty years old. Let me now bid a cheerful adieu to my youth. My young days are now surely over, and why should I regret them? Were I never to grow old I might be always here, and might never bid farewell to sin and sorrow. Lord, teach thy servant to rejoice in the hope of thy glory.

"*Saturday, July 13.* — Sir W. W. W. and Mr and Mrs S. and Mr C., came. Prayed that my affairs might be ordered for me, and that the duties of to-morrow might not be interrupted.

"*Sunday, 14.* — All our visitors went away before breakfast, except Mr C., who is almost no interruption to my devotions. Prayed in the morning with much thankfulness. God is my helper in every time of need.

"*Friday, 26.* — Read with pleasure, and saw my adoption from the character of the children of God. How great is my privilege! I would not resign it for worlds.

"*Sunday, 28.* — Meditated with pleasure on the Divine

disposal of all my concerns.

"*Saturday, Aug. 3.* — Mr Campbell and Wilhelmina* here. Happy to find dear W. still pious as I remember her. Meditated with pleasure on the goodness of God to her and to me, and to all His people. Oh! how does He heal our backslidings and forgive us freely!

"*Monday, 5.* — Had a long conversation with Wilhelmina at night on religious subjects.

"*Sunday, 18.* — Heard the children. — made me happy by saying she often forbore doing what she thought displeasing to God, and that she prayed for His Spirit every day. Prayed for them all with much earnestness, and with thankfulness for every serious impression.

"*Tuesday, Sept. 3.* — The light of God's countenance restored. Convinced that I would be heard by my gracious Lord, from considering that, when on earth, He never rejected any one who applied to Him for either temporal or spiritual blessings.

"*Friday, Nov. 1.* — Forgave an injury, in order to follow Christ.

"*Saturday, July 25,* 1812. — Read on the religious education of children; which led me, with my whole soul, to pray for God's blessing on my endeavours to bring up mine in the ways of piety. He knows my almost only wish for them is directed to this end.

"*Thursday, Sept. 24.* — Mr Millar and his friend, Mr Gorham,* here. Feel refreshed by the sight of this dear disciple of my Lord, though I had no opportunity of conversing with him on religious subjects.

---

* Sister of Sir James Colquhoun, and wife of John Campbell, Esq., of Stonefield.

* Since well known in consequence of the proceedings in the Ecclesiastical Courts of England.

"Friday, 25. — When it is so pleasant to meet with Christ's people here, think, O my soul, how delightful will be the society of heaven! Feel a desire to depart, but am grieved that I love my Lord no better. I long for more acquaintance with Him. However, I feel assured that I am His, and trust to His promise, that I shall one day be as I would. Did not resent an injury.

"Sunday, Feb. 7, 1813. — During the past week have got by degrees into a more comfortable frame, not from being sensible of any amendment in myself, but from trust in my Saviour, and from being sensible that I must rest in Him, sinful as I am. Feel very comfortable, and full of faith in the atonement of Christ. Resolved to endeavour never to think of myself any more, but to look on my salvation as finished, whatever my frame may be.

"April 4.* — In these duties not very lively, but have an abiding persuasion of acceptance through the righteousness and atonement of my all-righteous Saviour. Refreshed with the text, 'Whosoever receiveth whom I send receiveth me, and he that receiveth me receiveth Him that sent me.' Surely I joyfully receive and attend to the people of God. In the evening had a conversation with Sir James on religious subjects, which greatly pleased me. Oh! how are my prayers continually answered!

"25. — Walked alone. My meditation sweet. Among other things reflected with pleasure that, as every creature is placed in a situation most adapted to his wants, so surely that noblest work of God, the new creature, must and shall be one day placed where it shall grow and flourish. Oh! that I were thus transplanted; for this world is indeed a barren soil.

* After this period Lady Colquhoun usually wrote in her Journal only once a week, viz., on each Sabbath. Unless, therefore, the day of the week be mentioned, the reader will understand that it was the Lord's-day.

"*Aug. 15.* — Went to Church at Bonhill, there being no sermon at Luss. One part of Mr Gregor's discourse struck me. Speaking of our justification, he said, 'that the people of God, or believers in Christ, are really as much in a state of acceptance *as their Lord Himself:* He being their Surety, all their debt is paid, and there is nothing to object against them.'

"*Sept. 19.* — For some months have been led continually to meditate on death, and anxiously to wish that I could look with outstretched neck to the time of my dismission. My fears of it begin to abate. I feel heartily willing to leave the world, which, except for my friends in it, has no attraction to me. What principally staggers me is, that I do not sufficiently love my Lord, and long to be with Him.

"*Edinburgh, Feb. 13,* 1814. — Got a tooth extracted yesterday; and one thing which influenced me was the desire to attend the house of my God to-day. The gum was still painful when exposed to air; however, I resolved to go and hear Dr Buchanan. Refreshed by the sermon, though sometimes in much pain. One remark comforted me — that love to our Christian brethren is a sure sign of being Christ's disciples; as mentioned more than once in the Bible. I do, indeed, with my whole heart, love them.

"*Rossdhu, April 10.* — We all returned safe home last week, accompanied by Hannah, and Mr Proudfoot,* who conducted family worship, which I wished to establish, and we are to have it every Sabbath evening. I hope it may turn out for the good of us all.

"*June 26.* — No sermon at Luss. Heard Sir James read one. Went out and meditated on the love of Christ, and His frequent exhortations to faith. Oh! that I could

* Then tutor of her sons, afterwards Minister of Arrochar.

not doubt, and then I might say to this mountain of sin, 'Be thou removed, and it should be done', and nothing should be impossible to me. Well I trust my Lord has undertaken to cure my hard heart.

"*July 24.* — Impressed with the shortness of my abode in this world, which is to me a reviving, as well as awful idea. Indeed, I would not live here always.

"*Sept. 4.* — In the past week Hannah left me, and I parted with her and with my father and Lady Sinclair with more regret, as they are shortly going to England to reside, and I can see comparatively little of them. But shall I not trust to my Lord that all is right and well? I know that this dispensation is for good for me and us all, and I would not alter it.

"*Edinburgh, Jan. 15,* 1815. — St. George's in the morning, and heard Mr Thomson. At the Canongate in the afternoon, and heard Dr Buchanan, Ps. cxvi. 16. He concluded with a few advices to those who were determined to serve the Lord :— '1. Beware of self-confidence. 2. Beware of sloth. 3. Beware of worldly-mindedness. 4. Mix not too much with the world. 5. Be constant and fervent in prayer. 6. Be sure you trust in the mediation of Christ, and in Him only.' Oh! what means of grace do I here enjoy, for which in some periods of my life I would have given anything. As yet, little temptation has befallen me throughout the week. Have found benefit by realizing the presence of Christ when in the world. Were He, indeed, visibly there, how little should I care for others!

"*Feb. 5.* — At Mr Grey's chapel in the afternoon. He preached on the forgiveness of injuries. By the help of grace, resolved to practise this difficult duty in its fullest extent. I trust I am not utterly a stranger to it.

"*12.* — In the past week put in practice, as far as

possible, my intentions as to forgiveness. Think Mr Grey's
sermon was designed for my good, as I had much to try
me in many little things, which are sometimes as difficult
to overlook as greater matters.

"*March 26.* — After dinner we made an attempt to
hear Mr Chalmers, but the crowd was so great we could
not. Felt disappointed, particularly as it is my last opportunity here; but was soon reconciled. I have more need
to go home and meditate and pray. Did so, and my heart,
from being dead, became alive to God.

"*Rossdhu, April 23.* — Have of late been distressed
with the weakness of my faith, which cannot take Christ
at His word when He says that He will receive all who
come to Him. I can reason very well, that He could do
no more to show His willingness, and that we must buy
without money and without price; and yet I cannot feel
satisfied, because I do not love my Lord sufficiently.
What is this, however, but resting on my own perfor-
formances? And did I love Him as His dearest saint,
it would only be the work of His own Spirit, and He can
work it even in me. If not, I will endeavour to rest on
His naked word, that I am accepted in Him. This night
my faith firmer.

"*July 25, Tuesday.* — This day met with a trial of its
kind. Mrs Millar had given Mr Simeon, of Cambridge,
a letter of introduction to me. I should have been
delighted to see him, in hopes of getting some refreshment
from his conversation and prayers; but, from some accident, he went away before I knew of it : and although
I sent to Luss, I found he was gone. Of course, this was
ordered by my Heavenly Father; but I have found it hard
to be resigned. Lord, I hope I could be more easily
reconciled to temporal losses; but perhaps not. Oh! if
I may not receive help from men, be Thyself my light

and my salvation !

"*27, Thursday.* — The Lord has heard my prayer. This day Mr Proudfoot lent me 'Edwards on the Religious Affections'. On reading it I felt a stronger impression of the reality of Divine things, and of the infinite holiness and beauty of God and my Redeemer, than I recollect for very long. I now feel more certain of being His; have more love to Him; and (what makes me hope it is indeed His Spirit's influence) am more humble. Lord, I bless Thee for this refreshment. Thou hast seen fit to do Thy own work without any intercourse with creatures, and now I am resigned. Mrs Millar, in her last letter, mentions her meeting with Mr Simeon, who took leave of her in these words— 'God bless you. Commit yourself to Him. Keep Him in your heart. Remember there is no happiness without Him, either *here* or *in heaven.*'

"*Earnock House, Aug. 10.* — Have been here for some days, and have left Hannah at Polkemmet. Arose early this morning to read and pray. At church in the forenoon at Hamilton, and in the afternoon at Blantyre, when Dr Hodson gave us an excellent sermon on prayer, and the certainty of its prevalence if offered for things agreeable to the will of God. How often have I experienced this; and do I not now experience it? having prayed for the presence of God, and that I might hear His Word faithfully preached? I have met with the people of God in my journey, and Mr Millar has given me many religious books to read.

"*Rossdhu, Oct. 8.* — Prayed but coldly in private, but with fervour in the family. What a refreshment is family prayer, when my heart is dull, but longing for grace !

"*Edinburgh, Feb. 11,* 1816. — Not at church in the morning, having ear-ache. Have reason to be thankful for this complaint — it has kept me from two parties;

and the day before I took it I had heard of the great attainments of poor Bell (formerly my housemaid), who, amidst great bodily distress, has become eminently pious. I felt envious, and almost prayed that I might be made such by any means; but God soon taught me gratitude for the good health I enjoy. Pain is hard to be borne.

"*March 17.* — Another striking event among our connexions happened last week, in the sudden death of Lord Polkemmet. He had been long complaining, but was much in his usual way, when he dropped down and expired. Have been much with Mrs Baillie, and have tried to comfort her and raise her mind to God. I also saw the corpse — the first I ever saw. I felt no terror; but to me the sight was rather consolatory. I thought — Is this all death can do if we are Christ's? then, I will not fear it.

"*March 31.* — And now I am come to my last Sabbath in Edinburgh, and this day took leave of the dear pew in the Canongate Church, where my first religious impressions were awakened; for this spring the church is to be fitted up anew, and the seats altered. As I left it, could not help feeling— Thanks, thanks, O my God, that I ever sat there! Praised be my gracious Lord that I ever heard Dr Buchanan and sat under his ministry! Glory be to God, Father, Son, and Holy Spirit, that it was effectual to lead me to Him! Now I leave the means I so much love; nevertheless, I am continually with Thee. Thou wilt hold me by Thy right hand.

"*Rossdhu, April 14.*— Read Dr Colquhoun on 'Spiritual Comfort'. Think I enjoy what he describes as the lowest degree of it — a hope in the mercy of God through Christ, and a trust that everything shall be ordered for the best for me. How often have I wished for more! How have I longed for joy unspeakable and full of glory! But it is

all right and well ordered. My easy, comfortable life does
not require those supports which are afforded in pain
and suffering; and my weak heart would perhaps grow
vain if I were not often reminded that I am nothing and
can do nothing.

"*April 28.* — Sir James and his brother were ordained
elders. How truly did I join in the prayers which were
offered up for them! Last week I was much distressed
with the fear that my sweet ———— had formed an im-
proper acquaintance, and had got much attached to her.
After fervent prayer, spoke to her, with tears, on the
subject, and she gave me every satisfaction I could wish,
seeming willing to do what I pleased. Oh, my God!
protect my children! Make them Thine, early Thine,
for ever Thine! I ask nothing for them but in subservience
to this. My whole drift in their education has been
towards this end; but, Lord, Thou only canst give the
increase.

"*June 23.* — Was afraid of Lord and Lady ————
being here either to-day or next Sunday; but my God has
heard my prayers, and they are to come on Wednesday.
This week have the prospect of being four days following
in the world: have prayed for support. I feel the influence
of worldly company less hurtful than I once did, and can
lift up my heart to God in the midst of it much more
frequently.

"*July 18, Thursday.* — My dear Hannah arrived here
on Tuesday. I have reason for thankfulness that her life
is still spared. Oh that she may enjoy when here, and
while life lasts, the fulness of the blessing of the Gospel
of Christ! This is the fast-day preparatory to the Sacrament. This communion, I have little prospect from means,
as even Mr Gregor is not to be here. But I must endeavour to look from the dispensers to the ordinance.

"*19, Friday* (before the Communion). — Let me examine my evidences of faith in Christ. In the first place, I have no reliance on anything I have done, or can do, for acceptance with God. Secondly, I do trust in Christ alone for salvation; and, were I to die this moment, I should have no other plea before the throne but His life and His death. Thirdly, I have given myself up to Him, and am endeavouring to do His will and live to His glory; but 'faith works by love', and here the weakness of mine is very, very perceptible. O my Lord, how little do I love Thee! Yet, methinks, I must love Thee, when I can be satisfied with nothing without Thee, and when I almost think I could be satisfied with Thee, and with nothing else; when I love Thy image wherever I find it; and when I desire communion with Thee more than anything else. 'Faith purifies the heart'. Whatever defilement there may be, and undoubtedly is in mine, yet its desires are after purity; and surely I should not do justice to the work of the blessed Spirit, did I not think that it is more pure than once it was, or than it would have been without this gracious influence. 'Faith overcomes the world'. Here I can be more decided. The world? it is nothing to me; its pomps, its pleasures, its vanities — all nothing, nothing. Its cares are far less than they once were. Its sorrows I know not how I *may* feel, but I trust for Almighty support. Faith has overcome the world.

"*Sept. 29.* — My dear Hannah leaves me to-morrow. God only knows if we shall meet again; however, she (as well as I) belongs to Him, and it will be ordered for the best for us both.

"*Nov. 24.* — Read 'Life of Mrs Newell'. For some time past I have been in an uncommon state of mind, as I think, owing to one and another difficulty and trial. Feel in the strongest manner the importance of religion, and it is continually in my thoughts, and yet my affections seem dead. Read to the children both before and after dinner. Heard them, and prayed with them. Happy to hear them say that they had prayed alternately aloud in a room by themselves. Is not this some sign of good impressions?

"*Feb.* 2, 1817. — After dinner read to Sir James the 'Life of General Burn', a most interesting book. I feel quite happy here in my beloved retreat, away from the gay and busy world.*

"*May 4.* — Reading 'Doddridge's Lectures on Divinity', delighted to find some cases described as frequently occurring to Christians similar to my own experience. For instance, texts of Scripture occurring with power to the mind. Well do I recollect 'the deceitfulness of riches' occurring to me again and again, almost as if I had heard a voice, and when I could not recollect in what part of the Bible it occurs; and still the impression of it is fresh. Then, a strong persuasion of some particular request being granted, which removes from the spirit an overwhelming burden. Yes, my God, I know this case by experience. Thou hast seen me for weeks oppressed and groaning under what seemed a wound incurable, but Thy own sweet words, O Saviour! healed it — 'All things whatsoever ye ask in prayer, believing, ye shall receive'. Man, I knew, would tell me I must not take these words so literally; but I determined to credit God. I see no limitation, and I will make none; and never since have I doubted that I shall be heard. Some signs of it I already see. I seldom read this verse without tears, and the chapter containing it (Matthew xxi.) is dear to me.

* This winter was spent at Rossdhu. Her sons and their tutor were in Edinburgh.

"*May 8, Thursday*. — Mr Proudfoot was ordained Minister of Arrochar. And now, my God, who would not trust Thee? 'In the shadow of Thy wings will I make my refuge, until all calamities be overpast. I will cry unto God Most High, unto God *that performeth all things for me*.' I went up to Arrochar and witnessed the ordination. Mr Gregor conducted the service uncommonly well. His text was, 'Necessity is laid upon me : yea, woe is unto me if I preach not the Gospel.' The crowd was great, and he preached in the tent.

"*June 8*. — Read to Sir James, and prayed for a blessing. I never had more delightful views of the Lord Jesus than last night, in reading the parable of the good Samaritan. What a beautiful one it is! I could have kissed His sweet, compassionate, heavenly words. Art Thou, Lord, such a pure, glorious, gracious Being; and yet do I sometimes fear Thee as my enemy? Thou knowest the reason. Nothing but Thy Spirit can open mine eyes, and I will trust Thee that it shall be given. The most delightful view I can form of heaven itself is, that I shall love and serve Thee.

"*July 17, Thursday*. — This being the fast before our Sacrament, rose earlier and thought over my sins with penitence. How constantly do I sin in neglecting God — that God who is giving me so much to be grateful for! How constantly do I sin in my best works! However praiseworthy in the sight of men, every action is defiled with this disgusting quality. My most fervent prayers are tainted with this poison. My most self-denied labors for the good of others are sometimes rendered unworthy in the sight of God by pride. And how often am I far more gratified by thinking that a pious action will procure me the approbation of the dear disciples of my Lord, than of that Lord Himself! Oh! vanity, how dost thou

defile my almost every thought! And have I not been
envious? Am I clear of doing injury to the souls of my
dearest friends, and of all around me, by neglect? These
are a few of innumerable sins. 'Woe is me! for I am of
unclean lips, and dwell in the midst of a people of unclean
lips'; but let a coal from thine altar touch them, and take
my iniquity away.

"27. — Expected that Sir Gregory and Lady Way
would have been here to-day. Once, a sight of these
disciples would have been quite a refreshment to me;
now, through the goodness of God, I have much more
intercourse with His people. I suppose we shall see them
to-morrow.

"*Oct. 26.* — Dined out yesterday. All seemed to make
light of religion, or worse. I dared to put in *one word*
for it, and am happy to think I gain a little more courage
in this respect. Why — oh! why have I been taken out
and made separate? Why? but because God would be
a Father to me, and would have me for a daughter even
of the Lord Almighty! Oh! that He may dwell in me,
and walk in me, and be my God for ever and ever!"

Lady Colquhoun's Journals have left upon our mind
a delightful impression of sincerity and progress. Whilst,
on the one hand, there is no constructive effort to prove
against herself infirmities and sins with which she was
not chargeable; on the other hand, every significant
circumstance in her spiritual history, whether encouraging
or adverse, is detailed with scrupulous accuracy. And,
as the great end which she kept constantly in view was
self-improvement, she was not content with confiding to
these mnemonic pages her weekly portraiture, but against
detected faults she resolved and prayed and watched
until they were completely overcome. God gives grace to

the humble, and when, in later life, she perused these minute and ingenuous records, she must have been cheered by a thankful consciousness of expanding views and maturing character.

And should any reader of this narrative have adopted a similar plan for his own improvement, may we suggest that its entire value will depend on similar faithfulness? Apart from the haunting idea that it may fall into other hands, a diary will prove a snare if its writer tries to feel other people's feelings, and failing that, uses language in advance of his own experience. Like those piratical molluscs which take up their abode in the shells made by their neighbours, the religious professor who only prays or journalizes in other men's phrases will be sure to distort or dwarf his piety. And in the subject of this biography we see how much more growthful is a lowly commencement, if genuine, than the most brilliant beginnings, if made in borrowed exuviæ.

Although we have forborne from transcribing those passages in which a mother pours forth her desires and prayers, in the foregoing pages the reader has obtained occasional glimpses of her parental affection and assiduity. During this period her main employment was the education of her two daughters. With the exception of some branches, for which, whilst in Edinburgh, she called in the aid of masters, she taught them everything herself; and in the illusion of her own dear society her pupils never felt a task in any lesson. On the Sabbath evening they were joined by their three brothers, and the time was spent in repeating the catechism and hymns and psalms, and in hearing their mother read some book adapted to their years. Amongst her papers were found two letters, the one addressed to her sons and the other to her daughters. They are not dated, but must have

been written when her children were very young, and
when she had on her own mind the impression that she
might soon be taken from them :—

"My dearest James, and John, and William,

"I cannot leave you in this vain world without one
parting advice, and without once more assuring you how
dear you have ever been to me. Now that my body is
consigned to the grave, and my soul has returned to God
who gave it, to you, my dear children, it will not signify
whether you ever knew a mother's care or not, except
in so far as you profit by her counsel. Let me, therefore,
ask you, and let me beg that you would ask it of your
own consciences — Are you living to God? Are you
trusting in Christ for salvation, and obeying his commands?

"To promote this my every thought with regard to you
has been subservient. Were I assured of this, I should
feel comparatively easy as to everything else. Oh! my
children, this is the one thing needful.

"I feel a pleasing confidence that none of you are
ignorant of the method by which sinners obtain recon-
ciliation with God. I would, therefore, only urge your
immediate acceptance of Christ as your Saviour; of God
as your God. There is no impediment on God's part.
Blessed be His name, all His offers are free; be willing,
then, and you are His for evermore.

"How many temptations you must pass through I
tremble to think of; but I have an assurance, which I
would not part with for worlds, that my prayers for you
are heard, and will be answered, when I am sleeping in
the dust. I feel a hope that you will be blessings to the
circle in which you move, and that you will glorify God
by your conduct through life. What higher honour can

you aspire to!

"You, my dearest James, will probably have many opportunities of usefulness. If you live you will have much of this world's good things to dispose of; value them, I beseech you, only as giving you more of the power to do good. Oh! let all you are and all you have be devoted to God. Encourage every useful undertaking, and give liberally to the poor, as you have received liberally from God. Do all in your power to place pious clergymen in any church in which you may have influence, for this is a most important method of doing good.

"Should any of my dear boys think of entering the sacred profession of the ministry — Oh! consider the weight, the importance of the charge. Remember it is doubly incumbent upon you to be yourself what you exhort others to be. I charge you, my child, to preach Christ Jesus the Lord. Remember, if you do not use every means in your power to bring to the Saviour the souls of those committed to your charge, you are responsible for them.

"With one other advice I will conclude. I exhort you, my dear children, if any of you should at any future time think of marriage, that you will not allow beauty, or any outward accomplishments, to be the only thing you look for. In the choice of a wife seek for one who fears and loves God, and I will venture to assure you of happiness with her. Such a one in your own rank it may be more difficult to find; but among the families of the pious it is far from impossible. Pray to God, and He will direct your choice. I trust you will ever love and assist one another, and be dutiful and affectionate to your dear father.

"And now, O my God, shower down Thy grace in abundance on my children. Remember all my prayers for them; be to them what Thou hast been to me — I can ask no more. 'Save them from the evil that is in the world.' Grant, oh! grant that we may meet in glory, through the merits of thy well-beloved Son. Amen.

"I remain, your most attached Mother.

"Through life and in death,

"J. COLQUHOUN.

"Keep this letter by you, and occasionally read it over; when you are older you may understand it better."

The following are extracts from a similar letter addressed to her daughters :—

"My dearest Sarah and Helen,

"When this shall be put into your hands, I hope, my darling children, you will be in some degree reconciled to the loss it has pleased God you should sustain in the death of your most affectionate mother. I am sensible that it is a great loss to be deprived of a parent whose anxious care it was to bring you up in the fear of the Lord; and nothing could reconcile me to the thought of parting with you, but that I commit you to Him who has been my God in life and in death.

"And now, my children, when deprived of an earthly parent, to whom should you go but to your Heavenly Father? Believe me, there is in Him enough to make up for every loss, and much more than enough to satisfy every desire. Fall down on your knees before Him. Entreat Him to receive you. Entreat Him to be to you what He has been to your mother. Entreat Him to guide and instruct and sanctify you. And entreat Him, through the merits and righteousness of Christ Jesus, which, if you ask, are yours.

"Read the Bible carefully, and with a desire to be

instructed by it. And pray for a blessing on it. Read, also, other good books, many of which I leave behind me. Never neglect fervent prayer.

"My dearest Sarah, to you I leave my Diary, which you will find in my bureau, in the small place that locks inside of it. Let your brothers and sister see it; and I would recommend you all to keep one yourselves. I have found much benefit in doing so. By it you will judge what were my aims and desires. How far I fell short, God and myself only know. But you will also see, that I have trusted alone for acceptance in the 'Lamb of God, who taketh away the sins of the world'.

"Dearest Sarah, take some charge of your sister. Endeavour to instruct her in those truths in which I have instructed you, and by which she was perhaps too young to get much benefit. Try all methods to win her to the love and practice of religion; and if they fail, try them again. Be a mother to her, and God will bless your weak attempts.

"In whatever relation or station you may be placed, try to act as God would have you. Be very cautious of your friendships. Shun, as the plague, those who have not the fear of God, whatever other attractive qualities they may possess. Meet with such you must; but do not, oh! do not make them your friends. Whatever it may appear to you now, the time, be assured, is not far distant when death shall snatch you from everything here. Surely, my dearest girls, all my care, all my prayers for you shall not be in vain. Oh! then, dread the world; dread its follies, its gaieties, its company. Oh! then, place your happiness in religion. Oh! then, keep the commandments of God. Oh! fly to Christ for redemption. Do the angels rejoice when one sinner repenteth? and shall not my joy be unbounded to see my children saved with an everlasting salvation?

"With one more request I will conclude. My dears, do not mourn for me as those who have no hope. Look up. I am safe, I am happy, unspeakably happy. You may follow. All things are ready: Come to the wedding. Christ stretches forth His hand to save and support you; put forth yours and lean on the Beloved. 'The Spirit and the bride say, Come. And let him that is athirst come. And whosoever will, let him take of the water of life freely.'

"Let your brothers, and, if you like, your father, see this letter; and get a reading of theirs. Keep it by you, and let Helen have a copy. Be ever dutiful to your only remaining parent, and endeavour to prevent his feeling my loss.

"Farewell, till we meet (oh! may I not hope?) never to part, where we shall be ever with the Lord, ever with one another. My God, my Jesus, let thine everlasting protection shield my children from all evil. Save them, and they shall be saved. Make them holy and heavenly. I have endeavoured to lead them to Thee; receive them graciously, love them freely, and even in glory put a new song into my mouth — praise for the wonders of redeeming love to those dear as a right hand.

"I die, as I have lived,

"Your most anxiously attached mother,

"J. COLQUHOUN."

CHAPTER III

Remembering your work of faith, and labour of love, and patience of hope in our Lord Jesus Christ. — 1 Thess. i. 3.

> Therefore love and believe; for works will follow
>   spontaneous,
> Even as day does the sun; the right from the good is
>   an offspring,
> Love in a bodily shape; and Christian works are
>   no more than
> Animate love and faith, as flowers are the animate
>   spring-tide.
>   Longfellow.

HITHERTO the summers of Rossdhu had been often cheered by long visits from a beloved sister; but the last of these had now been paid, and, in the spring of 1818, that sister lay a dying invalid at Ham Common, in Surrey. There, besides the affectionate assiduities of her own family, she was favoured with occasional visits from a faithful minister of Christ, and the frequent society of an attached Christian friend. Lady Colquhoun could not come to her, but on this very account, her supplications were the more ceaseless, and her solicitude relieved itself in letters, which, for their sisterly tenderness and faithfulness, proved the chief cordial of the weary sufferer. In penning them the fond writer sought help from a Wonderful Counsellor; and, as they were full of His wisdom, as well as her own warm-heartedness, they always arrived like "words in season". Miss Sinclair kept them under her pillow, and used to have them often read over to her.

The following extracts from her Journal show how the mind of Lady Colquhoun was exercised during this anxious spring :—

"*Rossdhu, March 8,* 1818. — After church was quite overcome by receiving two or three lines from my dearest Hannah, written with great difficulty and in much weakness, but expressive of the composure of her mind and resignation to every issue. Oh! my God, I will praise Thee! Yes, I will praise Thee even in the fire of affliction, when thus tempered with mercy.

"*April 12.* — It has pleased the Lord to lay His afflicting hand upon me : but it has also pleased Him in great mercy to support me. I heard yesterday, that my dearest sister is no better, and getting still weaker. I have been agitated, but quite resigned; and I see so much, so very much mercy in every part of the dispensation, that I dare do nothing but lie quietly in the hand of God. After some thought, I wrote her a letter telling her of her danger. Oh! how was I puzzled how to frame it! but I trust my pen was guided by an invisible Hand. O Lord! accompany this bit of paper; be with her when she opens it; support her spirits; give her triumph in the thought of death! I trusted to Thee for direction; may it answer the end for which I wrote it! Employed much as usual to-day; but in the evening felt nervous and unwell. Still, I have the greatest possible confidence in the safety of the dear saint. I cannot mourn as those who have no hope, and I could not have believed that I should be so tranquil.

"*26.* — Oh! I am cold and dead at present. I am indeed worthless; my services worthless, my heart worthless. I feel some pleasure in writing these lines, and making this acknowledgment. In glory, and there alone,

shall I love and serve my God. And heaven is mine —
freely and without money, mine. Had not Christ died,
my portion were hell. Had the happiness yesterday to
hear that dear Hannah is no worse, and that Mr Gandy
and Miss Massie were to see her. How kindly is God
dealing with her; and thus He deals with all who are His.

"*May 10.* — Prayed with sincerity in the morning, and
laid all my burdens on my covenant God; for burdens
I have, and one very heavy to be borne. All hope is over.
Dear, dear Hannah is much worse, and I look for her
death every day. Still, Lord, Thou art faithful, Thou
art kind. Did not I pray for evidence as to her eternal
state? and is not my prayer fully answered? Is she not
everything I could wish? a pattern of meekness, patience,
long-suffering—faith? What would I have more? Must
she be detained from glory because I cannot part with
her? No, Lord! I would only still further implore that
Thy everlasting arms may enfold her now and for evermore; that her passage through the dark valley, which
is but a 'shadow', may be easy, and that Thou wouldst
be graciously pleased to support me, Thy poor afflicted
servant, and sanctify it to me.

"*17.* — Received a very gratifying letter from my sister
Catherine; not that my Hannah is getting better : my
dear saint must go to her blissful home; but I was gratified
with the affection expressed for her and me, and above
all, with the piety which appeared in it. *There* is the
fruit of my Hannah's labors.

"*24.* — My beloved sister still lives; at least, I have
not heard of her death. Oh! how hard it is to give up one
so truly dear : yet I feel resigned. My heart is sometimes
rent, especially when I hear anything of her affection for
me; but, in general, I am calm to a miracle. God has
done it. In this trying dispensation, how kind has He

been to me, warning me for eleven years of its approach, and at last taking her in the gentlest manner. I trust, too, it has already been sanctified. My heart has been raised to Jesus, and I have been enabled, in a faltering manner, to lean on the Beloved. Could I but know this dear Lord, I should trust Him.

"*Tuesday, 26.* — Hosanna! Hosanna in the highest! I have just heard that my beloved Hannah is in glory! What cause for praise! 'Unto Him that loved us, and washed us from our sins in His own blood, and hath made us kings and priests unto God, and His Father, to Him be glory and dominion for ever and ever. Amen.' Sweetest saint, thou art now far removed from me; but far, also, from sin and sorrow, and enjoying the presence and the smiles of Jesus. Oh, that my end may be peaceful, like thine! Not a fear disturbed thy serene composure, and thou slippedst gently away, as if afraid of disturbing others. Oh, my Hannah, hardly shall I find thy equal, as none can be equal to me! yet, could raising a finger bring thee back, I would not be so cruel. Though I must sojourn here a longer or shorter time without my darling sister, have we not an eternity to spend together? Let me rejoice in the thought. Oh, that I could raise this dead heart above the world! My God! sanctify this event to me, and accept my praise for Thy great kindness to the dear departed, and for so wonderfully supporting me.

"*31.* — Beloved Hannah! I would once more write a little to thy beloved memory. What a heart was thine! — filled with the desire of doing the will of God, and of conferring good on all around thee. Yet, hadst thou died some years ago, I should not have been so confident of the safety of thy state. God heard my prayers, and completely established thee in the faith, and now I have nothing to say but 'Alleluia: for the Lord God omnipotent

reigneth. Let us be glad and rejoice, and give honour to
Him : for the marriage of the Lamb is come, and His
wife hath made herself ready. And to her was granted
that she should be arrayed in fine linen : for the fine
linen is the righteousness of saints.' — Read to myself
and Sir James. Read to my children with much enlarge-
ment. At night prayed with tears. Even my prayers
distress me, for I used always to pray for my dear departed Hannah. I cannot omit her name, so I turn it
into thanksgivings for God's goodness to her."

The following letter was on this occasion written to
her sister's kind Christian friend, Miss Massie, of Kingston :—

"Rossdhu, May 30, 1818.

"My dear Madam, — I have delayed answering your
truly kind letter, till I was somewhat more composed,
after the heavy trial it has pleased my Heavenly Father
I should meet with. From the kind sympathy you express,
I think perhaps you may like to hear how I have borne
my loss. In this instance I can remarkably attest the
faithfulness of God. I have not indeed mourned as those
who have no hope. I never had but one anxiety for my
dear sister — and that, through mercy, is completely at
an end — 'that she might be found in Christ, not having
her own righteousness which is of the law'. I did, however,
hope to have seen her again; and from what she said
and the general strain of her letters of late, I hoped to
see grace grown in her, and herself fast ripening for glory.
Though I did not witness it, I have no doubt that this
was the case, and under God I attribute it to her intercourse with you, and to the ministrations of Mr Gandy,
in whose sermons she took great delight. I have no less
than six of these lying by me, which she condensed from

memory, and sent me that I might share the benefit. I
mention this, that you may inform that servant of God :
it may be some encouragement to him. I need hardly
add how much I was myself pleased with this, and how
highly gratified to think that she had the opportunity of
hearing such a man. I am much obliged by your account
of his visits to her. In every respect God has dealt kindly
with her : she wanted no temporal nor spiritual comfort.
It surely becomes me not only to say, 'Thy will be done',
but 'Thy name be praised'. She was one of my dearest
friends. We were educated together, and our hearts had
long been united; and I hope we are still united in Christ.
But must she be detained from glory, because *I* cannot
part with her? You say you have passed through the
same sad trial some years ago. Yes, my dear Madam,
but what will years soon appear to us? Are not those
that are gone already like a dream? Let us have patience
for a few more, perhaps a very few, and we shall meet
those friends who died in the Lord, never more to part.

"If I am not too troublesome, I would still request to
hear further about the dear departed. Anything will
interest me. I should also be glad to know if you think
my Hannah's life and death still continue to impress the
survivors.

"I remain, &c.

"It gives me much pleasure to find that a tract is to
be published, written by my sister, by which she 'being
dead will yet speak'. I long to have it, to distribute
among my poor neighbours."

Miss Sinclair died on the 22nd of May, and soon after
her death a little volume was published, containing her
own beautiful "Letter on the Principles of the Christian
Faith", and a brief memoir from Legh Richmond's happy

and descriptive pen. In its accessible pages the reader
may learn more fully how worthy was Hannah Sinclair
of her sister's devoted love, and how full of immortality
was the hope which sparkled amidst that sister's tears;
and it is only for us to add, how fraught with peaceful
fruits to the survivor was this long and deeply-felt affliction. These chapters may be read by some who have
sustained recent bereavements; if so, may their sorrow
in like manner be sanctified!

And, perhaps, the most natural effect of this trial on a
mind like hers, was the effect which Calvin's death produced on Beza— "Now is heaven more dear, and death
less dreadful". She had learned how lightsome the
Saviour can make the dark valley, and she almost wished
that she had traversed it when the "door of hope" opened
so wide, and let so much glory shine athwart it. And she
could think of the better country more vividly, because
one so familiar was there. To quote some of the simple
rhymes into which about this period her contemplations
often ran :—

> In sweet surprise that anthem swelling
>   With notes of joy and love;
> What seraph's form is this that treads
>   Jerusalem's courts above ?
>
> That form, methinks, I yet should know;
>   That heart, it once was mine;
> And still, my Hannah, does my soul
>   Unite in love to thine.
>
> Together from our earliest years,
>   In every thought united —
> Each in the other's grief downcast,
>   And th' other's joy delighted.

Oh! may we still such union prove,
And one in Christ be found :
And through one glad eternity
The Saviour's praise resound.

Arrayed in the deep mourning, which was little needed
to remind her of her loss, many were the solitary walks
she now took in the garden, and in the sequestered by-
paths of the "Policy"; and there, or seated on the margin
of the silvery lake, she loved to meditate on the multitude
before the throne; and just as in that multitude she recognised one dear as her own soul, for that dear one's sake
"the Lamb in the midst of the throne" became yet dearer.
Nor was it long till the sisterly thoughts, which used to
travel to England, as naturally ascended to heaven.

But along with this result came another, as important.
For many years she has ceased to live unto herself; but
up to this period her solicitude and self-denial had been
mainly for her husband, her children, and her immediate
family circle. This Providence, however, broke open a
door of exit, and bade her seek a wider sphere. She
received it as a personal message, and, admonished that
"the time is short", she looked eagerly around for opportunities of larger usefulness.

Accordingly, the first time that her neighbours saw
her, except at church, was at the formation of a Bible
Society, a few weeks after her bereavement. The day is
thus recorded in her Diary :—

"*Monday, June 29.* — I had the happiness of witnessing
the establishment of a Bible Society at Luss. It is to be
called 'The Luss and Arrochar Bible Society'. I hope I
was of some use in setting it a-going, though not the
original mover. O Lord, I rejoice to be in any way the
instrument of forwarding thy kingdom in the world, and
saving poor lost souls. With delight I heard Sir James

make a most excellent speech on accepting the office of President; and thus supported, I trust it may be a great benefit to the neighbourhood."

And from this time forward she devoted herself in more systematic efforts to the poor of her vicinity. And although the national reserve prevented her from gaining all the access she desired, or doing all the good she wished, her labors of love were generally appreciated, and she was conscious of a recompense in her own soul.

> " Blessed is he that *wisely* doth
> The poor man's case consider:"

So sings the Scottish version of the forty-first Psalm; and we have often heard that most enlightened of the poor man's friends, Dr Chalmers, quote it with applauding emphasis. And there was much "wisdom" in the way that Lady Colquhoun dealt with the "poor man's case". Amongst the natives of Luss she found Scottish pride in union with Celtic touchiness. Under the home-spun coat and Highland bonnet it was the same high mettle which often stalks in hungry magnificence beneath the Spanish cloak and sombrero, afraid of obligation, and affronted at alms-giving. "Na, na, I'm no in want," was the instinctive rejoinder of a tattered old woman, as a stranger slipped half-a-crown into her withered palm, which, however, as instinctively closed over the goodly coin, till the sense of want and the sense of honour were happily harmonized by some courteous word of explanation. And even after they consented to receive the gifts of indi- vidual kindness, it was a prime point of honour to owe nothing to public charity. One aged female, who was at last entirely supported by the Rossdhu family, used to place five pounds, the savings of a frugal life, beneath her pillow every night, lest by any possibility she might be chargeable to the parish for the expenses of her funeral. And another, who in extremity had accepted some relief from the poors' money, by her latter will provided that her personal property should be disposed of, and the proceeds refunded to the Session, and as the sale of her effects realized nearly forty shillings, it is likely that in her case the parish was no great loser. But grotesque as might be the occasional manifestations of this spirit, Lady Colquhoun respected and encouraged it. She was proud to know that her poor neighbours were not paupers, and, "considering their case", she bestirred her ingenuity how to relieve their wants, and save their independence. Amongst her pensioners was an aged and pious woman who formerly had charge of the poultry at Rossdhu. Her chief means of support was now derived from a humble class of lodgers, and the produce of a cow, the keep of which, along with her cottage, she had rent-free. She was also installed in the guardianship-general of the bee-hives, a post which entitled her to a small yearly stipend, and which only called for her attention in the pleasant hours of sunshine and summer. And when, at last, lingering infirmities left her long bed-ridden, her kind benefactress was constantly resorting to her cheerful but lowly chamber. There Lady Colquhoun confessed that she had learned many a lesson of gratitude and trust in God. Her joyful tribulation and patient hope were a visible sermon; and all the more instructive because derived from constant communion with heaven. Often when her visitor would draw near to her peaceful bedside and ask, "And what have you been doing, Nelly?" her answer would be, "My leddy, I've been wussin'."* One day Nelly's cottage was full of smoke, and on her entrance, Lady Colquhoun was greeted with the exclama-

* Wishing, i.e., praying.

tion, "Eh, my leddy! ye canna come in here for the reek, siccan a fine leddy as you." "Hold your peace, Nelly," was the answer; "when you and I are in the grave, if any person takes up your dust in one hand, and mine in the other, he won't be able to tell which was the lady." But amidst all this consciousness of the common humanity and the common frailty, there was an obvious elevation which commanded the respect, whilst it did not lessen the affection of the poorest. There was in her words enough of fellow-feeling to assure them of the speaker's friendship; but there was also that in her aspect which gave to these words the enforcement of a superior nature. And, surely, that is the truest grandeur which, even if station were lost or unsuspected, would still be noble, in virtue of its own refinement; just as that is the truest condescension which can lay aside everything except inherent dignity. So graceful were her manners, so delicate her cultured mind, and so lofty the homestead of her habitual thoughts, that, though she could forget or conceal the accidents of rank, she could never cease to be the Christian gentlewoman.

One day walking in the beautiful grounds of Park-place,* a picturesque cottage was pointed out to the writer, and he was told how, in the minds of some of the family, it was associated with Lady Colquhoun. In the course of her first visit, they were sauntering through the pleasure-grounds, when they came to that cottage, and she was asked if she would like to go in and see the aged gardener, then laid on his dying bed. She eagerly assented, and, after talking to him a little in her own sweet and engaging way, she begged her friends to continue their

* The seat of E. Fuller Maitland, Esq., near Henley-on-Thames. One of Mr Fuller Maitland's daughters was married to Lady Colquhoun's second son.

walk, for she could not speak so freely whilst they were present. By and by she joined them, radiant with that happiness which celestial natures feel when visits of mercy have been paid; and as the old man continually reverted to that interview, and the prayer with which it ended, as a sort of angelic epiphany in his homely history, we may hope that it was blessed to his everlasting benefit. And though it must be admitted that for such services she possessed a rare felicity, neither should it be forgotten that of that fitness the main element was her rare benevolence. Those who would fain be the benefactors of their brethren possess the main pre-requisites if they are blessed with warm hearts, and clear views of the Gospel; and for an open ear and a welcome they need not be anxious, if into the abodes of their neighbours they carry a bosom glowing with the Saviour's heavenly kindness.

In a tract, first published anonymously, Lady Colquhoun has supplied us with a specimen of her cottage conversations; and, as illustrative of herself and of the blessing which sometimes crowned her labors, we may copy a few paragraphs :—

"On my entrance I beheld an old man stretched upon a bed apparently in great pain, whose face was half eaten away by that dreadful disease, a cancer. Yet his countenance bore marks of intelligence, and of that cultivation of the mind, which, even among the lower orders, is so common in Scotland. His features were aquiline. He was pale and emaciated, and a certain wildness in his stare seemed to announce that he suffered greatly. The bed on which he lay was cased round with wood, excepting a space in front, by which to enter. The remaining furniture of the room consisted of another bed, a few wooden chairs, a table, and cupboard. The fire, which was of peat, burned upon the ground, without grate or chimney, the smoke seeking its exit through a small opening in the roof, which, however, seldom allowed of its entire escape. And a window, oft repaired, but dimly admitted the light of day. Yet this uncomfortable lodging, I am convinced, made no part of the misery of my new acquaintances; they had never known a better, and custom had completely reconciled them to the want of all the conveniences of life.

"I advanced towards the poor man, and said —

" 'I am sorry to hear you are so unwell.'

" 'Very bad,' was his reply.

" 'Are you in great pain? '

" 'Very great.'

" 'Does anything give you relief? '

" 'Nothing.'

" 'Are you always equally distressed? '

" 'No; sometimes the pain is much more intolerable; I could not speak to you if the fit came on now; but I shall never, never be better.'

"This last answer reminded me of the hint his wife had given as to the state of his mind.

" 'It is a consolation,' said I, 'to know that trials are sent for our benefit; and this one, hard as it is to bear, may prove a great blessing to you.'

" 'There is no blessing for me,' said he hastily; 'I am lost, undone, miserable here, and will be so, for ever.'

"As I gazed upon him, I saw despair pictured in his ghastly and disfigured countenance.

" 'I hope you are mistaken,' I replied. 'Do you not know that there is a Saviour for poor, lost, undone creatures? that He is able to save to the uttermost all who come unto God by Him; that He came to seek and to save that which was lost; and that He will in no wise cast out any who apply to Him for salvation? '

" 'I know all you can tell me,' said John, 'for I am
well acquainted with the Bible; but I know likewise that
there is no salvation for me.'

" 'Does any particular sin oppress your conscience?'
I inquired.

" 'No,' said he, 'I have lived a religious life. Unlike
many of my neighbours, I have kept the Sabbath —
prayed morning and evening — abstained from swearing
— attended on ordinances — thought I was serving God;
but He has rejected me; and this is a judgment sent from
heaven; it is the beginning of those pains which will last
eternally — it is hell begun.'

"I listened with horror as he spoke, for from the
expression of his countenance, his words, dreadful as
they were, seemed inadequate to convey his meaning."

For more than a year Lady Colquhoun continued to
visit assiduously her afflicted neighbour without seeing
any break in the gloomy cloud with which his soul was
enveloped. It was on a day when a grievous accident
had befallen his grand-daughter, who was the chief support
of himself and his aged partner, that the following conversation occurred :—

" 'Is it not a judgment now?' said he, on seeing me :
'would stroke upon stroke thus follow me if I was not
abandoned for ever — lost — going down to the pit? Oh,
the bottomless pit! it has a chain and key none can escape.
To be tormented day and night, for ever and ever!' —

"He would have proceeded, but I interrupted him by
saying, 'You have forgotten this text, "Whom the Lord
loveth he chasteneth, and scourgeth every son whom he
receiveth." '

" 'He will never receive me,' was the reply.

" 'John,' said I, 'you certainly labour under an unfor-
tunate delusion; it is necessary that I should examine

you a little more closely. Are you willing to accept of a full and of a free salvation? I know you will say that you are; but let me explain the meaning of these expressions.'

" 'To receive a free salvation means, that you accept of it without respect to anything on your part; that your past life has nothing to do with it, and that even your future life can have no effect in justifying you in the sight of God; that the life and the death of Christ are your only grounds of hope; and that you expect an eternity of happiness from Him, as a gift for which you can give no return.

" 'To receive a full salvation means, that you are willing to accept of the whole which Christ offers, salvation from the power of sin dwelling within you, as well as from hell. Jesus came to save His people *from*, not *in* their sins. Is there, then, anything which you know displeasing to God, but which you are unwilling to give up? any right hand you would not cut off, or right eye you would not pluck out? Christ addresses you as he did the man at the pool at Bethesda, "Wilt thou be made whole?" And the same Divine compassion is ready to be imparted to you that was exerted in his case. Any obstacle must be on your side; for the Gospel offers are without limitation.'

" 'O, God bless you! and He will bless you,' said John.

" 'I scarcely know any blessing,' I replied, 'that would afford me more satisfaction than to be useful to you. But consider what I have been saying; are you willing to accept of the salvation I have described?'

" 'Ask a man,' he answered, 'on the rack, if he will accept of relief; he cannot feel more anxious to obtain it than I am for the interest in Christ. I would do anything, everything, to know that I am His, and He mine.'

" 'Can you consent,' said I, 'to what is still harder to our proud natures, to trust in nothing that you *ever can do*, or *ever have done*, for justification in the sight of God; to let Christ have the undivided glory? His is a finished salvation; our part is to accept of it.'

" 'Oh, if I dared to hope!' said John.

" 'And why not?' I answered. 'Can any invitations be more universal than these, which are the words of our Lord Himself? — "Ask and ye shall receive; seek, and ye shall find; knock, and it shall be opened to you." "If any man thirst, let him come unto me and drink." "Him that cometh unto me, I will in no wise cast out." '

" 'I think I am under the influence of temptation,' said John, 'for I cannot hope.'

" 'No doubt you are,' I replied; 'but pray to Him who overcame the powers of darkness, and suffered being tempted, for strength to overcome the wicked one — to Him who in a sense above our comprehension could say, "Thou shalt not tempt the Lord thy God." I, too, will pray for you; and I feel inclined to trust that the cloud will at length be dispelled, and the Sun of Righteousness yet arise upon your soul, with healing under His wings.'

" 'Never was any one thus interested for my salvation,' said the old man.

" 'Ah! John,' said I, 'there *is* One who has shown Himself infinitely more interested for your salvation. If laying aside for a season the glories of divinity, living a life of persecution and distress, and dying a death of extreme anguish, both of soul and body, can prove it, the Son of God feels a solicitude to pluck sinners as brands out of the burning, to which no created being, in heaven or earth, is alive. And yet you fear to trust Him.'

"Tears gushed from the hollow eyes of poor John; he evidently felt the conclusiveness of my argument, and the

impossibility of reply. His countenance brightened — it
spoke volumes; but he uttered not a word. He appeared
for some time silently to feed upon the ray of hope which
had imperceptibly entered his benighted mind; he seemed
scarcely himself to credit that he entertained it, and yet
afraid to lose the first dawning of joy, to which he had
so long been a stranger.

"Oh, blessed Spirit! (I mentally prayed) enlighten his
darkened soul, irradiate it with thy bright beams, purify
it by thy benign influence; lead him to Jesus, teach him
how universal are the offers of Thy Word, and at length
may he find peace and rest in Thine everlasting arms."*

The day had now dawned, and soon the remaining
shadows fled away; and it was the privilege of his kind
instructress to know that his last days were irradiated
with a joy unspeakable and full of glory.

It was not till a later period that she was much in the
habit of visiting the poor in Edinburgh; but there was
one forlorn invalid there in whose case she felt much
interested. Bell Macintyre had been a housemaid at
Rossdhu, and was then a good-looking and a very
thoughtless girl. From Rossdhu she removed to a family
near Edinburgh, and was glad to find herself in that gay
neighbourhood; but in consequence of having swallowed
a needle, she was seized with an internal affection, acute
and lingering, and was never fit for service any more.
Her terrible suffering was aggravated by extreme penury;
and hearing that her first kind mistress was in town, she
sent her a message, which soon brought her to the
poverty-stricken chamber. But Lady Colquhoun was not
more affected by the sad alteration in her old servant's
outward lot, than delighted with the manifest change in
her character. In solitude, and often in great agony, the

* "Despair and Hope". By Lady Colquhoun.

Gospel was now her constant support; and, aided by a remarkable memory, she could repeat many long portions of Scripture, and turn to almost any passage, chapter and verse. Even accompanied by a servant, it needed some resolution to drive into the *close*, and climb the high and dirty stair at the top of which Bell usually lodged; but even into these repulsive abodes Lady Colquhoun was glad to find that philanthropy could penetrate. One day, whilst she was seated by Bell's bedside, two young ladies entered, smiled, placed sixpence on the table, and instantly withdrew. The sixpence appeared to be the stated gift of some kind benefactor, whose almoners these young ladies were; and their coming was a gleam of sunshine to which the poor sufferer could always look forward in her loneliness. And though Bell could never ascertain their names, for some time a young officer and his wife came daily from the Castle, and brought their sick neighbour her dinner, usually some delicacy in a covered dish, and waited till she ate it. But is it worth while to chronicle these little charities? It is worth while, inasmuch as Lady Colquhoun delighted to recount the kind deeds of other people. It is worth while, inasmuch as the dainty dish carried to the pain-worn prisoner may be noted in that Book where even the cup of cold water is recorded. And inasmuch as little charities, done in the Redeemer's name, are twigs of healing in the Marah of humanity — balm-drops on poverty's broken heart — it will be worth while, dear reader, if you and the writer go and do likewise. Bell had an only brother; he was a private in the forty-second Highlanders, and did not know of her distress. But as his detachment was under orders for Scotland, he sent his sister five pounds, that she might look smart and respectable when he arrived with his regiment. The letter was also accompanied with a present of his old military great-coat. When, at last, he arrived, he found her in a miserable lodging, and sitting up in bed, with his old great-coat wrapped round her. As long as he was quartered at the Castle he was very attentive to his sister; but he was soon sent abroad on foreign service, and Bell heard no more of him till tidings of his death were brought to her, accompanied by his watch and Waterloo medal. The watch was a great comfort during the solitary days and nights of nearly twenty years.

Every year on the estate of Luss an oak coppice or "hag" is felled, and in cutting it hundreds of labourers are employed during a portion of each summer. These congregate from all quarters, many of them being natives of the sister isle. And this, as well as the harvest-season, was an opportunity which Lady Colquhoun always improved for distributing tracts. Through the overseer, something could usually be ascertained regarding the previous history and character of each, and in this way he was presented with a word in season. The tracts were always received with avidity, and, besides being read on the Sabbath, they were usually carried away, perhaps to do good in distant places.

The Southern reader may have some difficulty in realizing such a state of matters; but many of our northern countrymen can still recall the period when the parish schools of Scotland comprehended the entire population. Partially endowed by the landed proprietors, it was their boast that they offered an education so thorough that the opulent did not disdain it; but withal so cheap, that the poorest could easily command it. Accordingly, with the exception of the principal gentry, who could afford a tutor, and the gipsies, to whose crepuscular habits day-schools were not congenial, the juvenility of the district all mustered at the same seat of learning, and in its playground the sons of farmers and weavers and ploughmen, the minister's laddie, and the bellman's heir-apparent, all kept their daily Saturnalia. Nor did any mischief result from this blending of various classes. Its chief tendency was to lay the foundation of a cordial and friendly feeling through subsequent life. And not only was this education unconscious of caste; it was catholic. Although intensely scriptural — within Presbyterian limits, at least, it was thoroughly unsectarian. The scholars were mighty in the Proverbs, and marvellous in the "proofs"; but we never heard of a parish school-master so misguided as to tamper with a denominational "testimony", or who taught young ideas to shoot in any ecclesiastical direction; but, sitting at his feet, little Churchmen and incipient Dissenters were closely united in catechetical alliance. And to crown this comprehension, brothers and sisters went to school together, learned the same lessons, and competed for the same prizes; so that traditions run of great authors, who, in their second lustrum, yielded the "writing medal" to some little dairy-maid; and more romantic traditions of undeveloped East India directors, who vainly strove for arithmetical precedence with the future Lady Mayoress. But although this system savoured of patriarchal simplicity, and tended to diffuse through the countryside a notable sense of neighbourhood, it was not without its drawbacks, and there was one which in her domiciliary visits, especially forced itself on Lady Colquhoun. She was sorry to remark the absence of neat arrangement and thrifty housekeeping in the surrounding cottages; and she felt that nothing effectual could be done for the in-door comfort of her neighbours till a girls' school was established. Opportunely for her object, a neat cottage, not far from

Rossdhu, was accidentally burned to the ground, and the occupants being provided with another abode, at considerable expense Lady Colquhoun rebuilt it, and fitted it up as a school-house. Neatly fenced, and the enclosure laid out in shrubbery, it became the type of that new order of things which she sought to introduce; and, attracted by a splendid fuschia, which nearly covered one gable, strangers and tourists often turned aside to visit the school. A suitable teacher was selected, and was sent to Edinburgh to perfect herself in needle-work, and to learn the most approved methods of teaching. Lady Colquhoun herself visited the school almost daily, and the severest penalty for misconduct was exclusion from the class which her Ladyship conducted. A striking improvement was soon perceptible in the district, and whilst the most casual observer could mark the softened manners and pleasing appearance of the scholars, the parents began to acknowledge their own advantage. Hitherto so little had the manual arts interfered with the abstract sciences in the education of their daughters, that few of them were able to sew, and consequently for the most rudimental essays in dressmaking they were obliged to call in professional assistance. It was, there-fore, a great surprise and satisfaction when they found that they had seamstresses nearly as accomplished in their own abodes.

Of course with the day-school was associated a Sabbath-school. To Lady Colquhoun her class became an object of ever-deepening interest, and by studying appropriate passages, and searching for memorable anecdotes and illustrations, she successfully laboured to make it attrac-tive to her pupils. As a teacher she had many advantages. Her voice was sweet and well modulated, her countenance benevolent, and her whole manner was full of engaging earnestness; so that she gained entire ascendancy over her scholars, and by the accounts which they received of her proceedings, many of the parents were induced to attend.

And she was not content with mere doctrinal instructions. She warned her youthful hearers against the sins to which they were actually exposed. And in many instances these affectionate persuasions succeeded. There was one bad custom in the West of Scotland at which she was especially grieved. It was the people's habit, after a marriage, a baptism, or a funeral, at the close of public worship, to invite their friends to the tavern, and there they regaled them with ardent spirits. Against this desecration of the Lord's-day, Lady Colquhoun set herself with all her might, and often alluded to it in her class. Her remonstrances were not without effect. Inveterate as the custom was, at the time of their own marriage some of her former scholars had courage to set it at nought, though others yielded; and it is to be feared that nothing except the spread of intelligence and piety will extirpate the disgraceful usage.

However, it is time that we allow the reader to return to that Journal in which Lady Colquhoun has undesignedly preserved her autobiography.

"*Saturday, July 18*, 1818 (before the Communion). — In time of worship there was an awful thunderstorm. How easily could God crush us worms! How shall we stand in that day when He shall be revealed in flaming fire? And how can any endure unless covered with the robe Himself hath wrought? Blessed Jesus! though most unworthy, I feel a confidence that I am complete in Thee.

"*Monday, 20* (after the Communion). — Mr Gregor preached on 1 Thess. iv. 13, 14 — to me a most affecting subject. I never was so overcome in church before. Every word pictured my dear, dear saint to my imagination. Many a pang do I feel when I think of her. Yes, my Hannah, I cannot easily give thee up. Oh, that name! How many times have I uttered it with delight; and often now do I repeat it — *sweet, sweet Hannah!* Dr and Mrs Buchanan were at church, and dined at the Manse, returning with us in the evening.

"*Aug. 16.* — My spirits for this little while have been low, I can hardly say whether from my recent loss or not; but the world appears dead to me, and my heavenly hopes less lively than within the last few weeks they were. I can hardly realize the thought of joy, even in heaven. Still, my beloved Lord lives, and my life is hid with Him in God. Thinking of God is the only refreshment I experience.

"*Sept. 13.* — This morning was much enlivened by Isaiah li. 11 — 'Therefore the redeemed of the Lord shall return, and come with singing unto Zion; and everlasting joy shall be upon their head : they shall obtain gladness and joy; and sorrow and mourning shall flee away.' Why have the redeemed this joy? It is because they 'obtain' it from God. Oh, the perfect, the everlasting joy to which they are introduced! May the thought of it make the trials of life sit lightly! Methinks, could I always view the promised land, even through ever so thick a veil, these crosses would not be weighty.

"*Nov. 1.* — Once more, within these few days, I have endeavoured to do every action only as I think God would have me. I have tried to ask myself, Is this what God at this time would desire me to do?

"*Wednesday, Dec. 2.* — Attended another meeting of the Luss and Arrochar Bible Society. It flourishes beyond my hopes. Nearly 30*l.* have been collected; and though there were not many present, there were more than for-

merly, and they seemed to enter into the spirit of it. All
the office-bearers spoke; Sir James twice, and he affected
me much, in particular when alluding to our Lord's
question to Peter, 'Lovest thou me?' What could I have
answered had it been addressed to me? Strange, that in
this I can never be decided; but if a desire to feed his
sheep be a sign, of that I am confident. Oh, prosper,
Lord, the means of spreading thy Gospel! 'Let the people
praise thee; let *all the people* praise thee. Amen, and
Amen. Then shall the earth yield her increase, and God,
even our own God, shall bless us!'

"*March 28*, 1819. — This day is memorable from two
interesting conversations; one with a dear friend, another
with a servant, to whom, along with the rest, I had given
tracts. Oh, for a blessing on my poor feeble endeavours!

"*May 9*. — Read in Scott's Commentary and a French
Bible. One passage in the latter (John xvii. 24) delighted
my heart. It strikes me as more impressive than the
English — 'Père, *mon desir est* touchant ceux que tu
m'as donnés, que là où je suis, ils y soient aussi avec moi.'
Is this the *desire* of my Lord? How much more should I
desire to be *with Him,* and where He is! And why, sweet
Jesus, dost thou desire to have me with Thee? From love
it must be — everlasting love! From a delight, too, in
the fruits of redemption; from seeing the travail of Thy
soul; from the satisfaction of beholding pollution pure.
And, doubtless, from the beneficent delight of carrying
forward the saints, even in glory, to higher degrees of
nearness to God, of holiness, of happiness.

"*May 23*. — 'Tis now a year since my beloved sister
has, I trust, been in glory. How differently has it been
spent from all her other years! How contemptuously,
perhaps, how wonderingly does she look down on the
many earthly things which might once have agitated the

mind! How pure are her thoughts! how delightful the
taste she has got of seraphic employments and entertain-
ments! and how overjoying the thought that they shall
never, never end! Oh, that we poor earthly pilgrims
could realize something of such scenes, and rejoice in the
hope of the glory of God!

"*June 20.* — Yesterday *my father in Christ*, worthy Dr
Buchanan, arrived here, and to-day he preached to us
from 1 John i. 7. It was a short but comprehensive
compendium of the Gospel. Was happy in hearing him,
and also much struck with his heavenly temper and
child-like confidence in God, combined with the largest
charity. How rare are such graces even in Christians!
Had a long and interesting conversation with him. Among
other things, he exhorted me never to let slip an opportunity of declaring my sentiments, and endeavouring to
do good, even to strangers. He also related several
instances where ejaculatory prayer had been remarkably
answered, and recommended its frequent use.

"*27.* — I was struck with the trustfulness, I might say
assurance, of Dr Buchanan in prayer; and recollecting
how much in every page of the Bible it is warranted to
the believer in Jesus, I resolved to dismiss my childish
fears, and trust in God as mine for evermore. It is
wonderful what an influence this belief has on the heart,
and how it prepares for the practice of those graces
which appear so beautiful in Dr Buchanan. Gave Boston's
'Fourfold State' to the servants as part of their little
library.

"*July 25.* — Afterwards heard my children — all my
children; and, I tremble to write it, our little circle may
never again meet in such circumstances. My beloved J.
and J. leave us this week for Mr Grainger's academy in
Lincolnshire, and if I am spared to see it, when they

return they may be beyond this mode of instruction. The precious moments are gone when a mother's warning voice might be heard with most effect. I have, indeed, this happy assurance, that if I could in any way have led my lambs to Christ, joyfully would I have done so; and that this was my first, and almost only ambition for them. And now would I commend them to God, and to the Word of His grace, which is able to build them up, and to give them an inheritance among them which are sanctified. Read to them Acts xx.

"*Sept. 19.* — Am at this time happily situated in the society of my Lord's dear children, dear to Him and dear to me. Mr Legh Richmond, who has been honoured to do so much good by his beautiful little tracts, came here last night, accompanied by one of his daughters, and another clergyman, Mr Westoby. They came in answer to prayer; my Lord has been loading me with benefits. Oh, how I love the fruits of the Spirit! there is nothing on earth can attract my regard *half so much*. With joy I beheld the image of my Lord shining brightly, and prayed fervently that these beauties may not only appear, but may flourish and abound in my whole life. Oh, that others might clearly discern that I had been with Jesus! At present I feel much encouraged and elevated. God is near. Have had some little trials, and do think I acted with regard to them as He would have me; and by prayer, and by trusting in Him *alone*, all was ordered for the very best.

"*Nov. 28.* — Last week I was reading the Life of Mrs Elizabeth Hamilton. She seems to have been amiable, and religiously inclined; but oh, I pity the person, of whatever talents possessed, who is not humbled at the foot of the Cross; and this, I fear, she was not. She talks of the greatest enjoyment in this life as being the society of persons of genius. Ah no! she knew not that other happiness, communion with God and His people. She speaks in raptures of Mr Alison's Sermon on the Talents, where he distinctly assigns a reward to the use we make of our intellectual powers, &c. A reward! For our services! It must be of grace, not of debt. But these things are often hid from the wise and prudent, and revealed to babes. Dazzling genius, how little canst thou do for thy possessor!

"*Edinburgh, March 12*, 1820. — In the evening I had my children, and read the Life of Pearce. When reading the lives of eminent Christians, I am pleased, but humbled. 'Less than the least of all saints', should be my motto. Without any affectation of humility, or the least intention of writing what it not *strictly true*, I see a very great disparity between the experience I read of, and what I feel. When believers complain, and mention how easily they yield to temptation, &c., I can say, This is my case; but when they speak of their joys, their raptures, their willingness to do, to be, or to suffer anything for Christ, their great love to Him, &c., my hands hang down, and I can only exclaim, Oh, that it were thus with me! Yet will I, too, hope in the Lord my righteousness. Let me be content to sit down in the lowest room, for so has He appointed.

"*Rossdhu, Aug. 20*, 1820. — My brother Alexander and sister Catherine are here. C. is to remain for some months. I prayed to be permitted to benefit her. What real delight it would give me! She gave me to-day the manuscript of my Hannah's 'Letter', which I read over this forenoon, and could have thought I was conversing with my earliest friend. It is, indeed, a wonderful production, and has scarcely any corrections for the press. This forenoon I also read the first portion of my Diary,

and was struck with the struggle against sin which appears
in it; was comforted by observing it, but almost fearful
that my watchfulness is not so great now. I do, however,
think that I have attained to an easier victory over some
sins, especially anger. Resolved and prayed to be enabled
to scrutinize my heart and life, more as a Christian ought;
to pass no fault unnoticed, to consider no evil trifling.
Spent this evening in reading, and hearing C. read.

"*Nov. 12.* — After dinner read in Romaine's 'Walk of
Faith'. He says that it is impossible to love God for His
holiness, without loving Him as our reconciled Father.
To myself it appears that I have done so; that the loveli-
ness of His character was a great means of leading me to
Christ. But probably I know not my own heart; at least,
I would with diffidence contradict so great a writer.

"*Royal Hotel, Edinburgh, Jan. 28,* 1821. — I should be
ashamed that any one of my fellow-Christians heard my
prayers, or knew how cold and indifferent they usually
are. And yet it truly does astonish me; God hears them.
In very many instances they have been answered, and I
hardly know an instance in which the rest may not be
answered yet. I must indeed remember that it is *through
Christ*, and I hope I feel that I have no other plea for
acceptance. When begging for any blessing with a cold
heart, I used to think, This prayer I cannot expect to be
heard; but now I can trust, wonderful as it is, that this
lifeless petition will find acceptance before the Throne.
Often have my prayers been brought to my remembrance
by their fulfilment.

"*Feb. 11.* — Heard Dr Stewart of the Canongate,
whom I have not heard since he was settled here. Was
much interested in the sermon, and in the preacher, who
is in very delicate health. May God spare and bless his
devoted servant!"

In the firmament of our Northern Church few names
shine brighter than that of Dr Alexander Stewart. Born
in the Manse of Blair, and spending his boyhood amidst
such romantic scenes as the Pass of Killicrankie, he
received an early tincture of that enthusiasm and poetic
fervor which make the Highlanders sublime; and then,
after a brilliant career in St. Andrew's University, by
ducal patronage he was softly deposited in the Manse of
Moulin. Just emerged from minority, and radiant with
life and hope, he could scarcely credit the rare felicity
which had landed him in this goodly preferment, all
unconscious of the probationer's usual fears and perils.
The Living was ample, the scenery delectable, the very
congregation was picturesque; and in the quiet of a
Scottish parsonage he could pursue those classical studies
to which he was powerfully attracted, as in the society
of an hospitable neighbourhood he could recreate his
spirit with the mirth or the music in which he equally
excelled. But all this while his heart was so little in his
sacred calling that it was a great relief when few people
came to his catechetical meetings, and from the most
solemn engagements he hurried away to the dance or the
novel. However, it was his great happiness to have for
his friend a minister so enlightened and fervent as Mr
Black, of St. Madoes. Impressed by his holy example,
Mr Stewart began to take more serious views of the
pastoral office, and longed to possess that piety which so
beautified his neighbour's character and so delightfully
inspired his labours. An affectionate intercourse commenced, and Mr Black's letters and conversations had
fully instructed in the way of God this young Apollos,
when, in June of 1796, Mr Simeon paid a short visit to
Moulin. Sufficient knowledge and an evangelical bias
he had already received, and the vivid words of his guest

were employed by the Spirit of God to impart His first joyful emotions. And now that the gracious principle, slowly elaborated but hitherto invisible, had received the spark celestial, it blazed up, a burning and a shining light. The conversion of Mr Stewart was followed by a remarkable awakening amongst his parishoners; and never did minister preach more powerfully than this ardent evangelist, never did hearers listen more wonderingly than these simple mountaineers. Its result was a revival, singular as occurring in the dullest age of the Scottish Church, and of which the many fruits are now ripening in places as remote as Cromarty and Calcutta.* After a translation to Dingwall, Dr Stewart was brought for the last months of his life to labor in Edinburgh. His earnest and richly scriptural sermons derived much additional impressiveness from his enfeebled and death-stricken looks; and during her remaining Sabbaths in town, Lady Colquhoun continued to wait on his ministry with mournful affection. And when, next year, his friend Dr Sieveright published his Life, it became her favorite book in Christian biography.

"*March 18.* — Oh, with what words of grateful acknowledgment shall I record the serious impression I have observed this day and lately in one very dear to me! I was delighted in conversation, and my hopes rise almost to confidence. I think and wonder at my prayer-hearing God. I can hardly in strong enough terms express my astonishment, I dare not say gratitude, though I do feel grateful, at the numberless answers to prayer I am daily receiving. Bless the Lord, O my soul!

* Dr Duff at Calcutta is a native of Moulin. Dr Stewart's eldest son, in many respects the most remarkable preacher in Scotland, lately died the Minister of Cromarty.

"*Rossdhu, April 22.* — Felt much interested in a plan which I this day began — reading aloud and explaining Doddridge's Rise and Progress to two of my maids, Mrs B. and G. Have long thought I neglected my duty towards them, in not myself explaining to them the doctrines of the Bible. Want of courage was the hinderance; but I resolved to begin with these two, who have been very long with me.

"*July 8.* — Read and prayed with all my children. Since the return of my sons my heart has been much engaged in prayer for them all. I began a new plan with them to-day — to get them to prove the various doctrines from the Bible direct.

"*15.* — To my great joy heard this day that Dr Chalmers will preach at Luss in September. May the Spirit of God bring home to my heart the truths he so forcibly preaches!

"*Aug. 5.* — The Sacrament Sabbath at Arrochar, and Sir James has gone there. May his heart be prepared according to the preparation of the sanctuary, and may he be benefited! A few days ago I received Mr Legh Richmond's Memoir of my Hannah — my dear Hannah. The delineation of her character is very complete; she *was* what is there described. I trust a blessing will attend it, and it gives me pleasure to think that I have had some hand in it. In many parts my words are retained, and I may thus be honoured to be useful without being seen.

"*Sept. 9.* — My God is gracious. I scarcely remember to have been favoured with so much of the society of His people as at present. ——— remained till Tuesday, and was succeeded by Mr Legh Richmond, his daughter, &c., and we had much agreeable and spiritual conversation. Mr Hamilton of Strathblane came here yesterday, and preached to-day. He is a faithful and able laborer

in God's vineyard. I delight in the saints, the excellent
of the earth, but it is out of their power to lead me to
God. The best society will not do without much retirement. I find deficiency in all. I would listen to the lesson
which I ought to deduce from these observations, to 'cease
from man'; I would learn to look forward with outstretched affections, to uninterrupted communion with
God, my God, my exceeding joy, and to intercourse with
the blessed without any mixture of defect.

"*Sept. 16.* — Again would I confirm what I wrote last
Sabbath; it is deeply impressed upon my mind. Emptiness,
insufficiency, is in the world, and in the world's inhabitants, and is even found in the people of God. Can we
expect spiritual light from creatures who are only in the
dawn of their spiritual existence? God *may* work, and
often does work by them; but when disappointment
occurs we need not wonder. Dr Chalmers preached here
to-day. In the pulpit his powers are certainly great, and
his reasoning very clear; but having heard that he is so
extraordinary, I was, on the whole, disappointed. Mr
Simeon's deep devotion and beautiful style impressed me
more. Though heard above twenty years ago, his sermons
are still written on my heart. Thanks, Lord, that I ever
heard them — that these affecting ordinances were
afforded to me when I so much required them! By the
remarks now made on communion with the saints I may
seem to contradict what I wrote Sept. 19, 1819. What I
mean is this. God may draw near, as Jesus drew near
the disciples going to Emmaus, and may bless intercourse
with His children; and then it becomes a delightful means
of grace: but He often does not, to disappoint their hopes
and lead them from the streams to the Fountain."

This extract is printed for the sake of its true and
important reflections, and all the rather, because these

are connected with a name transcendant amongst modern
preachers, and to which eventually none could pay more
cordial homage than Lady Colquhoun. But if this first
sermon did not fulfil all her expectations, perhaps it was
for a reason which, had she known it at the time, would
have only made him, to her pious mind, appear more
noble. His text was, "The common people heard him
gladly"; and, as was his wont on such occasions, he
would lay aside his grand originalities, and labor after
those obvious truths which common people are glad to
hear. The doctor always adverted to this visit with
peculiar pleasure; nor must we forget to add the delight
which it afforded to his new acquaintances at Rossdhu,
from the boatmen who rowed him on the lake, and the
little girl with whom he played at battledoor, up to the
guests whom he one evening dazzled with an astronomical
lecture, converting the dinner-table into an extempore
orrery, with a d'oyley for the sun, decanters for the
planets, and glasses for the moons. To Mr Simeon's
clear and vivacious sermons Lady Colquhoun had been
deeply indebted at the outset of her Christian course.
There was one particularly to which she often adverted.
The text was, "Ye will not come unto me that ye might
have life"; and after reading it the preacher, in his own
striking and peculiar manner, exclaimed, "Life? blessed
Lord! dost thou offer us life?" and in an instant en-
chaining the attention of his auditory, he kept it solemnly
rivetted to the close of his discourse.

"*Nov. 18.* — With much interest read and explained
to my maids. I have now had resolution to take them
all, and cannot but hope from their apparent attention,
that some benefit will accrue to them.

"*May 5*, 1822. — This Sabbath the influences of the
blessed Spirit appear to me more sensible and sweet;

genuine religion has more exercised its empire over my soul. I have lately been deeply humbled on account of heart sin, and last night in meditation had some realizing views of the necessity of salvation by Christ, and of His fitness to be a Saviour. To-day, in the morning prayed with sincerity and truth, and felt interested in church. Read three times aloud — to my young people, to my maids, and again at night, in the parlor. Felt pleasure in all, and longed and prayed for *some* fruit of my labor. Took a walk before tea, and spent an agreeable half-hour in meditation. Went to the family burying-place, and remembered those who are mouldering there, one of whom (Sir James's father) I had intimately known. Imagined my dear husband and myself consigned to this narrow cell, and tried to look forward to the resurrection, and consider what alone can make it a joyful day to me. For life and death commended myself to my Redeemer, whose protection alone can avail in the solemn scenes through which I must pass.

"*June 3.* — Was led to remember my fellow-worshippers at Halkirk. Their new pastor, Mr Munro, who has got the church from Sir James, so much to the satisfaction of the parish, was to preach there for the first time to-day. May the Lord the Spirit descend on pastor and people!"

For more than a year anterior to this date the health of Lady Colquhoun had been very delicate, and her allusions are frequent to that event which the most skilful physicians told her was its probable issue. In the prospect her feelings were calm, humble, and, although solemn, full of confidence in God.

"*Oct. 27*, 1822. — Last week I felt far from well, which has led me to consider the possibility of this complaint still finishing my earthly career. The thought has done me good, and the prospect has not been dark. I have been enabled to view Christ as my eternal portion, and nearly to give up all besides. I feel wonderfully reconciled to leaving my husband and children, and I know I shall die or live as God sees best for me. Dear Lord, thou art at all times managing for the best my little concerns. Last week, also, I had a most interesting private conversation with Miss Jane Farrell, who now appears a true disciple. I have seen her to-day, probably for the last time in this world, as she leaves Camstraddan on Tuesday for Ireland, and is shortly going to India, to be married. Well, in a future state 'there shall be no more sea'; nothing to divide the blessed inhabitants; nothing to interrupt their communion. I hope I have been of some use to this interesting girl."

Mr Farrell was proprietor of an estate near the Giant's Causeway, in Ireland; but his wife was in delicate health, and along with their three daughters they had resided for four or five summers at Camstraddan House, near Luss. Young ladies so well informed, and of manners so pleasing, were welcome visitors in most houses of that neighbourhood, and they were very often at Rossdhu. Miss Jane especially drew towards herself the affectionate observation of Lady Colquhoun. A prepossessing appearance, good sense, a cultivated mind, a warm heart, and frank and lively manners, made her a universal favorite; but, beyond a weekly attendance at the parish church, she gave no evidence of an interest in the things of God. And even this church-going was a mere formality. "Have you remarked that picturesque old woman who on Sundays sits on the pulpit stairs?" she one day asked her friends at Rossdhu. Of course they had. "Oh!" said the amateur artist, "she is such a fine-looking old woman, I cannot take my eyes off her the whole time of the sermon, and I am painting her likeness from memory. I can carry away each Sunday an impression of her features sufficient to employ my pencil during the week." But, in conjunction with other circumstances, the prospect of leaving home solemnized her mind, and led her to ask whether, separated from all the means of grace, her religion had strength to stand? and this led to another question — whether she had any religion at all? A severe mental conflict ensued, and at the time when her thoughts were all engrossed with these anxious questions, at a dinner-party she met Lady Colquhoun. On leaving the dining-room the ladies went out to walk round the garden. Lady Colquhoun and Miss Jane Farrell having separated from the rest, in her own sweet and engaging manner Lady Colquhoun introduced the subject of religion, and her young companion opened to her all her mind. After this their interviews were frequent, and as they were the principal means of leading this interesting inquirer into the light of the Gospel, they originated an ardent and life-long attachment. "Her last visit," says our informant, "is still fresh on my memory. It was a bright autumnal morning, and I well remember her light and elegant form, as she glided along the avenue, after bidding farewell to her friend and adviser." In company with Sir Edward and Lady Barnes she sailed for Ceylon, and was married to her brother's partner, Charles Scott, Esq. From her home among the cinnamon-groves she wrote to her friend on Loch Lomond letters brimming over with the fulness of her own felicity, mingled with occasional misgivings as to her spiritual progress. "I possess great earthly happiness. I hear of my beloved family being in excellent health, and have the prospect

of rejoining them in a very few years; and I have one of
the kindest and most indulgent husbands that ever lived.
But all these blessings, instead of raising my heart in
thankfulness to the Giver of every good, and leading me
to devote myself more to His service, seem only to bind
my thoughts more firmly to this world; and I am often
made to fear that I shall be deprived of some of those
great mercies I am so unworthy of possessing. Yet no
contrition seems to accompany the knowledge of my own
sinfulness, and I have generally a gaiety and happiness
of heart which should only be produced by the hope of
daily advancing in meetness for the kingdom of heaven.
When my prayers are cold and wandering, I feel I cannot
deplore it as I ought, nor do I ask with sufficient earnestness for assistance to pray better; at the same time, I
certainly do often feel the indescribable happiness of
being able to trust in One mighty to save, and that it is
not for our sakes that our prayers are accepted by God.
I think I am gaining rather more knowledge of my sinfulness, and of the waywardness of my heart; but, as I said
before, it is unaccompanied by sorrow for my offences,
and does not diminish that lightness of mind which is
certainly gaining on me." It was thus that Lady Colquhoun's gentle and guileless nature drew forth the confidence of her younger friends especially, and encouraged
them to tell her "all that was in their heart"; for they
were as sure of kind sympathy as of wise advice. And,
perhaps, the fears of her ingenuous correspondent were
not without foundation. God may have seen what she
herself suspected, and in order to bring the roaming
spirit back into its quiet rest, he sent the wintry storm
and the tempest. Six weeks after these lines were written,
Mr Scott was seized by a fatal malady, and in a few hours
it tore him from the arms of his distracted wife. A

devoted missionary, Mr Mayor, heard of her distress, and along with Mrs Mayor, the beloved sister of a man greatly beloved — the late Rev. E. Bickersteth, prevailed on her to come for a season to their calm and secluded abode. There she gradually regained composure — at least serenity enough to benefit by the conversation and prayers of her deeply sympathizing friends; and when, in 1828, she returned to her native land, although she brought with her a heavy load of sorrow, she also brought a mind uncommonly devoted to God. From Dublin, on February 13, 1829, she thus wrote to Lady Colquhoun :—

"I have often intended writing to you. In the time of my deepest affliction, you were one of the very few my heart seemed to turn to, feeling that you would understand where consolation can alone be found. I have indeed been in a strong fire of affliction since I last wrote to you. Oh! that the fire had consumed more of the dross. *Then* I was at the height of earthly happiness. The fall was sudden and violent, and unless upheld by an Almighty arm, I must have perished in my affliction. On the first shock I was left to my own strength, and the mind wandered under the acuteness of anguish. It seemed as if I could not pray; yet even the first look to Him whose compassions fail not, was answered, and in a way I could not have conceived before. I was made to experience my own inability to have so much as one thought, except by the help of God, and His wondrous power to shed into the soul the richest spiritual consolations in the midst of nature's woe. Oh, the deep, deep, almost overpowering views then given me of the vastness of eternity; and great in proportion was the consolation, when, by the tender mercy of God, there came back on the mind the transporting conviction that the soul, which

seemed the dearer part of my own, was entered on an
eternity of blessedness — that, as surely as Christ died
and rose again, even so them also that sleep in Jesus will
God bring with Him. And the evidence that his state was
such, was so abundant, as to raise my soul in wonder and
gratitude. My earthly, back-sliding heart had been so
satisfied with present happiness as to be comparatively
forgetful of spiritual; but now I remember with indescribable comfort, these last seven or eight months in
particular, the gradual, the beautiful change, that often
made me exclaim to myself, 'I may have more of religion
on my lips, but he has infinitely more of it in his heart.'
The sting of my many omissions, in regard to his spiritual
welfare, I thought at first could never be extracted; but
my compassionate God has been pleased long to remove
it, and even change it into an additional motive of
gratitude to Him who did it all Himself, and who did not
allow my sinfulness to come in the way of the great work
of His salvation."

Then, after mentioning Mr Mayor's providential visit
to her dying husband, and her sojourn in the house of
the missionary and his "truly Christian wife", she con-
cludes :—

"My voyage was such as to keep faith in constant
exercise — many dangers, but a powerful, protecting
God appearing through all. I may humbly say, 'Hitherto
hath the Lord helped me.' I am continually made to
feel my weakness. Were I trying to look to earth, in any
shape, for comfort, the heart would yet entirely sink
under sorrow. But, blessed be our faithful God, who will
never leave nor forsake us; who can give us faith to rest
in His promises; and who can show the blessed termina-
tion, when those sundered on earth shall unite for ever

in praising redeeming love. My dear Lady Colquhoun, I have given you a letter filled about myself; but I know you will join with me in praising the mercy and love of our Saviour God. Your letter was indeed most comfortable to me. I received one from you at Badda-ganna, written when you thought me in the midst of earthly happiness. I was struck by your saying in it: 'If we cannot give our hearts to God, let us pray that He will take them — by any means take them.' You had little idea then that it required my best earthly treasure to be taken to heaven before I could feel that my *all* was there."

The eighteen years of her widowhood were spent in a succession of ministrations to one invalid or afflicted relation after another, which in several instances appear to have been blessed to their everlasting salvation. At last, in the year 1845, and when she hoped to see again her spiritual parent, the Lord called her to Himself. She said, when dying, "I had too much stress on the ministry of man, and delighted in it. I cannot now converse but with difficulty. God is drawing me off from all earthly props that I may lean solely on Himself. How abundantly I felt the promise fulfilled last night! The Comforter, the Holy Ghost, was indeed sent, and abundant was the supply of Scripture brought to my remembrance. Not merely what I had committed to memory, but large portions that I had not, came pouring in to comfort me." And as God had taught her to live upon Himself, so she was very fearful of being too highly exalted, or too much spoken of by others. A diary which she had kept she destroyed before her death, and when told that a friend had written to inquire how she was, and how she had felt supported, she said, "I can so well understand Mr

Simeon's feelings,"* and, like him, she for a moment or two waxed quite eloquent in extolling her Saviour, and disparaging herself; and like him also she silently departed, telling her attendant to keep the room quiet, for she was going to sleep.

Thus, on earth they never met again, and in the many thoughts which followed her to her Indian bungalow, her Irish home, and her cottage on the brink of Niagara, in the fancy of her friend it was always the same Jane Farrell. And though the widow's garb was worn, and though many griefs and watchings by sick-beds had doubtless changed that pleasant countenance, no change came over that ardent, ingenuous, and self-devoting mind. And down to the close of life Mrs Scott retained a fervent attachment to Lady Colquhoun, and in her letters fondly reverted to the happy days when "first she knew the Lord", and when they were wont to take sweet counsel together. "Dear, dear Lady Colquhoun, I have indeed often thanked God for having given me such a Christian friend. When my mind was awakening, you were the first that spoke home to me. You first directed me plainly to Jesus, and encouraged me with the assurances that He would carry on the work which He alone could commence. And, dear friend, what increasing comfort there

* "He was evidently much hurt at the thought of even his dearest friends coming round to disturb the privacy which he had always wished for in his dying hour. He had repeatedly charged me to keep every one away from him when that solemn season should arrive, and remain with him myself alone. * * * Next morning he referred to what had happened the previous night. 'Now, I was much hurt at the scene last night : a scene! *a death-bed scene I abhor from my inmost soul.* No!' he continued, smiting three times slowly on his breast, 'No; I am, I know, the chief of sinners; and I hope for nothing but the mercy of God in Christ Jesus to life eternal; and I shall be, if not the greatest monument of God's mercy in heaven, yet the very next to it; for I know of none greater'." — *Carus' Life of Simeon*, p. 810.

is in that view, grounded on God's own Word, that He will perfect that which concerneth us, and will not forsake the work of His own hands. What a God we have! God in Christ. Truly you say, 'The end of our trials is to endear to us Jesus, and loose our hold of everything else.' " Of these trials the meek writer had many, and one was the loss of the letters addressed to her by her endeared correspondent. During a sojourn at Kingston, Upper Canada, the house in which she was residing was burnt to the ground, and we cannot forbear inserting a portion of the letter in which she describes the calamity, April 8, 1837 :—

"You kindly said you would send me 'The Kingdom of God'. All my efforts to procure it have been vain, and, alas! its beautiful sister, which I prized so much, is gone. Where? Like many other fair and lovely things, to dust and ashes. We were living in greater comfort than I ever expected to meet in Canada; too much at ease, no doubt; when one night a fire broke out below us. The flames spread rapidly, and all our worldly goods were consumed. It was night; the house, of course, in total darkness, and all sound asleep, till wakened by loud cries of 'Fire!' Our rooms were at the greatest distance from the hall, and worst situated for escape. The fire originated in a hardware store under the boarding-house, and when we got outside the house we heard there was gunpowder in the store sufficient to blow it up. Two explosions there were; but they did no additional harm. So there we stood, in the snow, watching the fierce flames forking up from our rooms, so shortly before the picture of peace and comfort. Nothing could be done, and the whole of it was so ordered that one could only offer it up into His hands who can make all things work together for good, and pray that we might effectually learn the lessons it was meant to teach. Besides much valuable property, I have lost all my books and written papers and letters, my Indian things, with all mementoes of beloved friends and past times. Another hint to forget the things which are behind, and press forward. But why do I thus detail our little losses? I meant *not* to do it. Rather let me speak of the great gain, the ever-increasing comfort of the promises, and of our Lord's love, who in every trial condescends to speak such peace as raises the heart to Himself in continual thanksgiving. When I think of what I deserve I can only wonder at His gentle dealings. He often says, 'What I do thou knowest not now, but thou shalt know hereafter'; and He graciously lets so much of His hand of love be seen in every trial, that it is easy work to trust Him with the remainder."

Of the many letters which Lady Colquhoun addressed to this younger sister "in the kingdom and patience of Jesus Christ", we are thus precluded from offering to the reader any specimen. But even this slight record of so dear a friend may reflect some light on the character of Lady Colquhoun. It shows, at least, how alert she was for opportunities of doing good, and how graciously God honoured her consistency and prospered her fidelity. Nor will it be a vain digression if it enkindle in the reader or the writer aspirations after that heavenly-mindedness and holy skill which made the subject of this biography a living epistle, and which so frequently converted morning calls and evening visits into "walks of usefulness".

CHAPTER IV

No chastening for the present seemeth to be joyous, but grievous:
nevertheless afterward it yieldeth the peaceable fruit of righteousness unto them which are exercised thereby. — Heb. xii. 11.

What causes the freshness which gives the flower
 Its scent and its summer hue ?
It came in the dark and midnight hour
 In drops of heavenly dew :
So, often in sorrow the soul receives
 An influence from above,
Which beauty, and sweetness, and freshness gives
 To patience, and faith, and love.

Edmeston.

THE last extract from her Journal represented Lady
Colquhoun as suffering from enfeebled health. This
trial was of long continuance; but it was sanctified. It
turned her thoughts more stedfastly towards that world
of which she thought it likely that she might so soon be
an inhabitant, and it roused her to make more efforts
for the good of that one which she was leaving. Amongst
other plans of usefulness was one which, abruptly suggested, would have startled her diffident and retiring
nature; but the idea stole on her so gently, and the process
went on so imperceptibly, that almost before she saw it
formidable, she found it a fact accomplished. During
those languid months when debarred from active employments, she might often be observed seated on her camp-
stool, beside the lake, or in some sheltered spot, and with

her pencil tracing her meditation as it rose. And as such papers grew upon her hands, and she felt some pleasure in perusing them, the thought occurred that in a connected form other people might read them, and might haply derive some profit. And she liked the scheme all the rather when she thought how isolated she was — how few, comparatively, came within her personal influence, and how seldom, even to those few, she could talk on the things importing their eternal peace. So that this expedient of addressing them anonymously in little books seemed quite the plan for doing all the good and shunning all the notoriety.

Her first publication was the tract to which reference has already been made.* With that scrupulosity which strikingly distinguished her character, it was entitled "A Narrative founded on Fact". Although every particular was stated with all the accuracy of an excellent memory, yet, as she had taken no notes at the time, and could not answer for every turn of expression which occurs in the dialogue, she thought it needful to insert this qualification. The story is not only essentially true, but it is an affecting record of God's grace. It will be read with much advantage by those who are in the habit of visiting their poor and afflicted neighbours, and we believe that it has been the means of conveying to some troubled spirits light and comfort.

Next year, viz., in 1823, appeared "Thoughts on the Religious Profession and Defective Practice of the Higher Classes of Society in Scotland. By a Lady." This little volume she wrote with an especial eye to her own personal acquaintances; and though it did not excite general attention, under her *incognita* she was frequently cheered by knowing that it had fallen into the very hands for

* "Despair and Hope". See pp 56-61.

which she designed it, and that in some cases beneficial results had followed.

This encouraged her to give to the world, in 1825, "Impressions of the Heart, relative to the Nature and Excellence of Genuine Religion". Even in its nameless disguise this work was widely circulated, and from its good sense and high-toned spirituality, along with the refinement of taste and delicacy of feeling which it everywhere betokened, many of her personal friends suspected the authoress. And its popularity has not exceeded its merits. Of that artistic skill which makes the most of materials, and which, in the pages of some celebrated female essayists, brings out effects so brilliant, Lady Colquhoun was nowise ambitious; and here and there it would be easy for an ordinary critic to balance the antithesis more nicely, or nib into a sharper paradox the pungent aphorism. But to a higher order of readers these beautiful essays bear a special charm, by reason of their graceful ease and natural truthfulness. Like the conversation of the compiler, they are genuine and in-artificial, spontaneous and heartfelt; but still the utterance of a mind whose every tendency is upward, whose every association is with things pure and good and elevated. And in such chapters as "The Invisible Mark", "Cease ye from Man", "The Ascent of the Mountain", "The Celestial Visitant", and "The Multitude before the Throne", we are persuaded that all congenial minds will eagerly respond to the devotional fervor, the bright but chastened fancy, and the holy fidelity in which the gifted authoress has so well transcribed herself. Calm, cheerful, Christ-loving, no book could be more rightly named than these "Impressions of the Heart"; for, according to the Indian's definition of writing, she who penned them has "pressed her soul on paper".

"*Edinburgh, 117, George-street, Jan.* 19, 1823. — After dinner, being unable to read aloud from my cough, I had a most interesting conversation with a very dear friend, for whom I prayed with tears and faith. Since last Sabbath, and indeed before it, I have been remarkably happy in my devotional exercises. I have secured more time for them, and have been confined at home, my cold hindering me from going to several parties. I have also been busily employed in a work that seems strange to myself. Early last summer my little book was published, and has met with acceptance; I even heard one instance in which it had been beneficial; praised be God! And I am now attempting something on a larger scale, though whether or not it will see the light, I cannot tell. But I have been earnest in my prayers for direction and assistance, which encourages me to hope it may be blessed. Amen.

"*March 2.* — Again detained at home by cough, which has never entirely left me since coming here. My frame has been far from lively; but I have had some feeling thoughts of *my wants.* Read Traill's Works with great pleasure; they are full of spiritual food. *My book* came out last week. I have prayed to be kept out of sight, and to be honoured as an instrument in the hand of God. Who knows what good may be done? I have also prayed to be kept humble if it should meet with any approbation, and I am not sensible of any elation regarding it. If it should pass with little notice it could do me no harm.

"*23.* — Attended in the Canongate and in St. George's, and heard two excellent sermons. Mr Thomson's, on the value of the Scriptures, was very striking. The duties of the evening were performed as usual, and at night I *really* prayed. This day has been comfortable; but last week I was much in company, and I seem as unable as

ever to withstand its influence. I am almost weary of
repeating my conviction of guilt, of weakness, or earthli-
ness; but each day proves it, and every period of my life.
In town I fancy I should be better in the country; in the
country I imagine a change of means would enliven me.
No. It is *myself* I would fly from. O wretched being,
who shall deliver me! I thank God, through Jesus Christ,
my Lord.

"*Rossdhu, June 1.* — One great cause of complaint
with regard to myself I think is, that I live too little upon
Christ. I could not live without Him; but I forget my
need of daily and hourly supplies from His hand of support and grace. I forget to ask His aid, not merely
formally in the morning, but often, and as my necessities
arise. I forget to hold with Him continual intercourse of
prayer and praise; in short, to live by His constant bounty,
as the Israelites lived by the heavenly manna. — It has
given me no small concern to find that I am suspected
by some as the author of my last little work; but I have
entreated my Lord to manage for me everything con-
cerning it, and I am confident He will.

"*8.* — No sermon at Luss, being the Sacrament at
Bonhill. Have, during the forenoon, been very happy in
reading and prayer, and in conversation with Sir James
on the great and glorious events which we are led by
prophecy to anticipate as very near. In all probability
we shall be laid in the grave before the time is fulfilled;
but still the prospect is cheering, that the kingdoms of
this world shall become the kingdoms of the Lord and
His Christ.

"*22.* — Thanks be to His mercy, the love of Christ —
that long-wished-for grace — of late has dawned upon
my heart. I have been more alive to my Saviour's beauty,
and have felt my dependence upon Him for everythlng,

alike for one moment's comfort, and for the happiness of a whole eternity. My intercourse and communion with Him have been sweeter, and I can cast on His care myself and all my concerns. I feel the inferiority of creature love. Amen; thus be it to Thy poor worthless child more and more, dear Lord!

"*July 13.* — Since last Sabbath a powerful temptation has occurred to my mind, and damped my joy. It was first impressed upon me that our Lord is not equal with God the Father; but after searching my Bible, this text set me at rest regarding that point, 'Making himself equal with God', an inference which He does not deny, John v. 18. But here my spiritual adversary did not rest; for being relieved as to that point I was next tempted to doubt the truth of revelation. Sad was my heart for some days as I labored to recollect the evidences that the Scriptures are divinely inspired. I felt that Satan was envious of my hope in God, and strove to destroy it; and yet doubt would force itself on my mind. If I had no God on whom to rest, all was lost. Among other books, 'Watson's Apology' has been of use in leading me to see the reasonableness of belief in Jesus. That the facts recorded in the Bible are true, profane as well as sacred history testifies; and if these are true, Christianity is true. O Lord, confirm my weak and wavering faith!

"*13.* — My faith is confirmed. The proofs from prophecy, from miracles, from the life of Christ, from the tendency of the Gospel, and many others, are indeed satisfactory. And now, O Lord, what wait I for? my hope is in thy Word.

"*20.* — Communion Sabbath. — When I consider the price paid for our redemption, how marvellous is the theme! So familiar to our thoughts has it become that we can scarcely reflect on the amazing truth that God suffered to save us. O may I for ever live to praise Him! He suffered in no slight measure, but intensely, and with the natural dread and aversion from agony that we all feel; yet calmly, resolutely, and with the dignity which His divinity alone could inspire.

"*Aug. 31.* — Death has made an inroad on my real friends. My old and faithful servant, Morris,* has gone to her eternal rest, full of days, at the age of eighty. She brought up my beloved Hannah and me, not only with care and affection, but with an endeavour to lead us in the paths of piety. I rejoice to think that we were a comfort to her in her declining years. And now I alone am left of our nursery circle. Both the departed have gone, I trust to glory. Oh may I follow!

"*Oct. 5.* — Have to complain to-day of a lifeless heart. What a difference is there between the duties of religion as performed when the blessed Spirit enlightens, warms, and purifies, and when all is the outward act! I hope, however, I am not wrong in relying on the Saviour for acceptance, even in performing duties such as these. He is perfect, and through His sacrifice and righteousness my poor services will, I trust, be pardoned and received. In going to church I saw a melancholy scene. The excessive rain of last night had flooded whole fields of corn, and in some places the sheaves had floated into the lake, and the poor people were trying to save them.

"*117, George-street, Edinburgh, Feb.* 15, 1824. — Oh how shall I praise the Lord for His goodness! Last week I was much in company, and alas, alas! I much forgot my God. But hearing that this was the communion Sabbath in the Canongate Chapel, though without the possibility of devoting any time to preparation, I resolved to attend, and never did I enjoy more of the presence of

* See p 6.

God at His table. Oh! He is kind, He is gracious to a poor, weak, inconsistent, lifeless creature. Every word of Mr Tait's exhortation reached my heart. He exhorted us, first to remember our transgressions, our shortcomings in duty, our unworthiness. I thought, I am sure this is for me. But having wounded he healed, and next pronounced the mourner 'blessed'. He then exhorted us to expect largely, for here God smells a sweet savour in Christ crucified; and he concluded by enforcing holiness — yea, to shine with the lustre of holiness, while we exhibit the depth of humility. Returning home, I prayed to my exalted High Priest with very much feeling, giving myself entirely up to Him, and imploring His blessing on me and my family for evermore. In the evening I read to my young people and servant with pleasure, and all the day have felt near to God, united to Him in covenant, complete in Christ.

"*Rossdhu, Sept. 5.* — Last Lord's-day I was in Edinburgh, having gone for medical advice. . . . Attended St. George's with benefit; but, alas! I have to record an act of transgression in return for the Lord's mercy towards me. I was living at the British Hotel, and Mrs ———— asked me to dine with her after sermon. We never accept invitations on Sabbath; but somehow I agreed, as we were to remain only two days in Edinburgh, and the following one was to be spent with my father's family. It did not occur to me that I had done wrong, till I found how the evening was employed, and then all the objections to my going occurred in full force; my own loss of spiritual feeling; example to others; the remark of one asked to meet me, but who did not come, and which stung me to the quick— 'I am sure I may do what Lady C. does'; besides the employment of servants in preparation, &c. O Lord, pardon this wilful offence, and may I never thus spend thy holy day again!

"*Oct. 17.* — Being employed last week in some deeds of mercy, rejoiced to think that such was the frequent employment of my Lord. Was delighted in reviewing His character, and longed for greater assimilation to it.

"*Nov. 21.* — Have been again in Edinburgh. Went with Sir James to witness my sister Julia's marriage to Lord Glasgow, an event which gives satisfaction to the whole family. May it be blessed to their everlasting good! It was the time of the Edinburgh sacrament. I attended in St. George's, and was pleased, but I fear not much edified. This day, at home, with no means but my book, my heart has been with God.

"*4, Charlotte-square, Edinburgh, Jan. 16*, 1825. — I have been weak and low, and prevented last Sabbath from writing here; but I cried unto the Lord and showed before Him my trouble, and He listened to my supplication. To-day have been twice to St. George's, and particularly blessed in the afternoon: the sermon upon 'abounding more and more in religion'. My intended work, 'Impressions of the Heart', is in the press. Oh for a blessing upon it! Lord, hear my many prayers for this! Let it find acceptance with the world. Give it access, not only to the closets, but to the hearts of thy people. It is indeed much to ask from a means so inconsiderable; but, Lord, make it extensively useful.

"*Feb. 6.* — On Friday, accompanied by Sir James, my brother George, Mrs Sinclair, &c., drank tea with Dr Colquhoun of Leith. It was truly affecting to hear the venerable man discourse on prayer and other religious topics. He gave me and mine his fullest blessing, and I was refreshed by the visit."

As has already been noticed, Dr Colquhoun was a native of Luss, and, of course, a member of the clan.

For nearly fifty years he was minister of the New Kirk, Leith; and to his solid and systematic expositions of Scripture hearers resorted not only from the city of Edinburgh, but from places as remote as Dalkeith and Newbattle. Besides Boston and the Erskines, his theological models were Witsius and Mæstricht, Voetius and Cloppenburg, and his own mind had all the system and precision of a Dutch Divine. No modern better merited the title so often bestowed on the Puritans — "a painful preacher of the holy Gospel". His expositions were ready-made commentaries, and every sermon was a chapter in a forthcoming treatise, whilst his deliberate enunciation, like an audible typography, rendered ample justice to every italic, dot, and hyphen. It would, however, be a great mistake to fancy that he was a mere systematist. Much as they valued his methodical arrangement and exhaustive copiousness, the best of his hearers prized still more his affectionate applications of the truth, and the singular judgment with which he handled questions of conscience. And in the midst of his mild catholicity, to many there was a peculiar charm in his covenanting fervor. Some of them can still remember with what pathos he used to pray that the Most High "would revive the credit of a covenanted work of reformation, that He would repair the carved work of the sanctuary, which had been broken down, and build up the breaches of Zion, which are wide as the sea"; and they can tell how, in concluding an exposition of the Psalms which had lasted seventeen years, he remarked, "I have much reason to bless the Lord that I have never, like many of my brethren, been so far left to myself as to use in the public worship of God hymns of human composition."*

* It must be regretted that, in common with so many distinguished ministers of the Church of Scotland, Dr Colquhoun has

Except in theological soundness, the minister named in the next paragraph was a great contrast to Dr Colquhoun. The fair, soft countenance, surmounted by its sleek, yellow wig, the measured tones and quiet air of the outer man, were in true keeping with the phlegmatic temper of the South-Leith divine; and as true an index of his lofty idealism and sanguine thorough-going, were the tall form, the brilliant but pensive eye, the nervous gait, and the impassioned address which marked the pastor of Strathblane. By nature a recluse, and rejoicing in a splendid library, his philanthropy and his love of freedom drew him frequently into public life, and eventually health and life were lavished in efforts to break up the religious apathy of a singularly callous neighbourhood. With peculiar emotion the writer sometimes recalls those magnificent exhibitions of redeeming love with which his own boyhood was familiar, and wonders how, like his fellow-parishioners, he was so little thrilled by their grandeur, so little softened by their tenderness. To Lady Colquhoun, however, these attributes of the ardent evangelist were a sufficient attraction; and, after the death of Dr Buchanan, the minister who enjoyed most of her friendship was Dr Hamilton. And it is only

passed away without any tribute to his memory. The natural repositories — the religious magazines of the country, are vainly searched for fuller notices. In the "Christian Instructor", vol. xxvi., p. 860, two of the most remarkable ministers of that day are thus disposed of :—

"Died, 28th Oct. (1827) the Rev. Dr Thomas Davidson, of Muirhouse, one of the ministers of Tolbooth Church, Edinburgh, in the 81st year of his age, and 57th of his ministry.

"27th November, the Rev. Dr John Colquhoun, Minister of the Chapel of Ease, Leith, in the 80th year of his age and 46th of his ministry."

For the above notice of Dr Colquhoun the Editor is indebted to his esteemed friend, Mr Rowan, of the Free College Library, Edinburgh.

because her fittest biographer died before her, that another pays to her Ladyship's memory this tribute of inherited respect and attachment.

"*March 13.* — Have been much in the society of the pious during the past week, and it has been blessed to me. I had an unexpected call from Dr Hamilton of Strathblane, which gave me great pleasure. He wishes that I should give my name to the next edition. Oh! what *shall* I, what *should* I do? Lord, take it or not as Thou wilt, and may my fears, or perhaps vanity, be quite excluded. I would stand by, as having nothing to say in the decision. Let Thy glory and Thy pleasure be the rule, and influence my mind according to these. On Tuesday was at a delightful meeting for the Irish. On Thursday heard Dr Gordon preach a charity sermon for diffusing religious knowledge among the poor. Friday dined with my brother George, and met Mr Wynne, and some others; and yesterday George took me to call for Lady Carnegie. All these advantages have not been entirely lost upon me, but have been the means of raising my heart to God. Oh how delightful will be the society of heaven, ever with one another, and ever with the Lord!

"*Rossdhu, July 17.* — Our communion. My mercies are new and my feelings varied. In the first place, I have been greatly hindered in heart-work by bodily weakness. When I would pray, I incline to sleep; and I have been greatly exhausted both to-day and yesterday. Surely my Lord, my own Lord Jesus, who was Himself united to humanity, knows this. Would a kind father say to a worn-out child, Get up and work? May I not rather hope that the Redeemer's language to me is, 'the spirit is willing, but the flesh is weak?' Nevertheless, I *did* come to Christ, and I did hope in Him; and I do feel some love to my adorable Saviour. With something of joyful anticipation I look forward to being with Him for ever. Here, I am labouring to catch a spark or two of celestial fire; but oh! to have it blazing around me, enlightening and warming my whole affections in the paradise above!

"*May 28*, 1826. — (Beginning a new volume of the MS. journal). My life wears apace! My appointed time is running on, years roll over and are gone. Where are those with the occurrences of which I filled my last little volume? They have fled; but the remembrance of them lives not only in that little book, but in the mind of the eternal God. Each thought and every action is present with Him, even as if it were only passing now. Then what a poor creature do I appear! and how rich is His mercy in compassionating and blessing such! I commence this book : shall I finish it? or shall this hand be arrested by death, and shall these fingers be consigned to the grave to mix with their native earth? Lord, thou knowest. But whatever awaits Thy child, be present, my God, to cheer, to support, to strengthen, to sanctify, to glorify. Amen. Sir James has been absent about a fortnight, attending the General Assembly, of which he is for the first time a member.

"*July 9*. — Oh how great is thy goodness towards them that fear Thee! towards them that hope in Thy mercy! Thou hast refreshed the soul of Thy poor weak servant, my God! Last week we had the happiness of a visit for some days from Mr Malan of Geneva, with whom James resided for a year. He is a most devoted servant of God and has been the instrument of arousing, and I hope confirming, my too wavering faith. He dwells much on the necessity of assurance, and even appears to think it essential to saving faith. In this last I cannot agree with him; but I am convinced we doubt when we ought not.

Wherefore doubt? Is it not the truth of God that we
doubt? Perhaps our sins are the cause. Well, cleave
the closer to the Saviour; we shall not fall away if He
upholds us. Or, we are not sure that we have come to
Christ. Then come now. To-day I am unable to attend
the house of prayer; but oh! how sweet were my morning
hours, when all the family were at church. Surely, Lord,
Thy dear servant who was lately here cried mightily unto
thee for me, and Thou hast heard his petitions. Present
Thou wast, even as if I had seen Thee with me. I read
the eighty-sixth and eighty-ninth Psalms. In the latter I
read that 'in thy righteousness I am exalted'. The
righteousness of God! noble thought! clothed with this,
how perfect am I! where can blemish be found? I read
that 'Thou, Lord, art my strength'. Then I shall never,
never forsake Thee, but go on from strength to strength.
I read that 'Thou, Lord, art my defence'. Then evil
cannot assail me. No, what I think evil is good; God
stands between me and all harm. Let that barrier be
broken, if it be possible! I read, 'The Holy One of
Israel is my King, and help is laid on One that is mighty'.
Oh! what a King! Dear Lord, Thou art mighty, Thou art
holy; I will fight under Thy banner; I will rejoice in Thy
name all the day long.

"*Edinburgh, Feb. 11*, 1827. — Have once more heard
good Dr Marshman preach from Romans xii. 1. Had
likewise the pleasure of meeting him at my brother's
house last week. With my heart I gave him the right
hand of fellowship. We may never meet again on earth,
as he is going very soon again to India, to live and die
in his Master's service there; but I trust we shall meet
in the multitude of the redeemed around the throne. My
prayers ascend for him that he may be supported in
whatever trials he is called to endure, and that after

turning many to righteousness he may shine as the stars for ever and ever.

"*Rossdhu, July 22*, 1827. — A sweet day this, for though not in His temple, I saw the beauty of my King. I was prevented going from indisposition, which however did not prevent enjoying myself at home. I sat by the water's edge, and in my little summer-house, with the Bible; and the loveliness of Jesus never appeared to me more apparent. How kind, how gracious His words! I save been thinking a good deal on the doctrine of assurance, of which much is said since Dr Malan's visit to Scotland. It appears to me plain that assurance is perfectly warrantable in any sincere believer, and ought perhaps to be more pressed upon such, than is often done; but I *cannot* exclude all who have it not. It is a grace, a gift, and is not given to all; and I do believe that saving faith exists without it. Does not our Lord himself speak of weak faith, accompanied by doubting? (Matt. xiv. 31). I feel, however, that unbelief is sinful, and do indeed hope, and am confident of being myself accepted, freely, for *His* name's sake. Mrs Baillie and my sister M. are here.

"*Edinburgh Feb. 3*, 1828. — Mr Tait's sermon was from these words, 'O Israel, thou shalt not be forgotten of me', and it did me good. Oh the height and the depth of the love of God! I have not been forgotten of Him; not forgotten in youth, not forgotten in trial, in care, in sickness; not forgotten when sinning, and *forgetting* God. Nor shall my little unimportant concerns be forgotten while I live; nor shall I be forgotten to eternity! Precious promise! for days of sore trial may come, but if God remembers His poor child they shall be mitigated. And none of my prayers are forgotten. Lord, I would acknowledge when I have myself forgotten them, thou hast often brought them to my recollection by granting their petitions.

"*March 30.* — In the evening went to my brother George's, where Mr Mejanel discoursed on the type of the Brazen Serpent. We had a little conversation on prayer, and he is almost the only person I have found who seems completely to have my own views on the subject; that 'all things *whatsoever* we ask in prayer, *believing*, we shall receive'. I know not what words to use stronger or clearer than the language of this delightful promise; and why is it not credited? Mr M. said that real Christians are warranted to expect assuredly an answer to every prayer which they can offer without doubting of its success; because this confidence is given by the Spirit of God; because His Word declares that when they pray believing, they receive their petitions; and because they will not be permitted by God *thus* to ask and yet ask amiss. By many this would be thought presumption or enthusiasm; but it has long been my belief, founded on experience and the promises."

Here we interrupt the Diary to make room for a letter written to the Rev. A. Westoby, of Emberton, Bucks. The man of God to whom it chiefly relates imparts to it a peculiar interest.

"*Rossdhu, Sept. 4,* 1828.

"Dear Sir,— I am happy to say that Mr Richmond's 'Memoirs' have at length arrived safely. I was anxious about them, feeling responsible to those who subscribed through me. As you asked my opinion of the work, I delayed writing till I had read it. I have been very much pleased, and I think edified, by the perusal of it.

"It is well written throughout, and Mr Richmond's character I have no doubt is justly portrayed. Indeed, from what I knew of him, I could see *the man* in every page, which led me to take a deeper interest in all that he said and did. He was blessed with a heart of no ordinary dimensions, which was his principal characteristic, and which, when sanctified by grace, made no ordinary Christian.

"The mention of my much-loved sister Hannah's 'Memoir and Letter' having been useful, is of course gratifying to me. It has been so, I have reason to hope, in very many instances. My introduction to Mr Richmond, at Rossdhu House, when you were present, for the purpose of writing an account of her life, seems now like a curious dream, and is one of those unforeseen events which Providence is often bringing to pass for His own glory.

"I cannot help noticing how much I was pleased with Mr Grimshawe's observations on the Apocryphal question. Oh, that there was more of 'the dove-like spirit' diffused among us! To me it appears clear that our friends on this side of the Tweed are in the right, but I exceedingly lament the acrimonious spirit on both sides.

"The Rev. Dr Thomson of Edinburgh has, I think, made a noble stand for the diffusion of the *pure Bible*, and his name will probably be handed down to posterity in this connexion. What a pity that there should be anything to regret in his manner of urging that the Word of God should keep its exalted station, distinct and separated from all human composition! He is in private life most amiable, and any heat of temper is, I am told, never seen at home.

"The doubts Mr Richmond seemed to experience, as he drew near his end, are likewise, I think, an additional refutation of a doctrine on which a few, and but a few, of our northern clergy have lately insisted, viz., that

assurance is a test of faith. If we exclude such a man as
he was, we shall make the boundaries of the Redeemer's
kingdom narrow indeed. It is, however, certain that faith
for the time is weak when doubts exist. I was reminded
of a conversation I heard between Mr Proudfoot of
Arrochar and Mr Richmond. The fifth chapter of Romans
had been read at family worship. Mr P. asked Mr R.
what he would say to one who there was every reason to
think was justified by faith, but who had *not* peace with
God? 'I would search a little deeper,' said Mr R. 'There
must be a defect in faith, if it does not produce peace.
Faith when in exercise always does.' The approach of
death will, no doubt, lead us to sift the reality of our
hopes to the foundation. May that foundation be Christ!
How true that most of us while we live are but 'half-
awake!'

"My paper leaves me no room to say more.

"I remain truly yours,

" J. COLQUHOUN."

"*18, Circus, Edinburgh, April 5*, 1829. — This is the
last Sabbath previous to my beloved ————'s leaving
me. I feel strangely in the prospect of her being removed
from my care, and sorrowfully when I think of the days
that are past, her infant years as well as those when she
has been my sweet and cheerful companion. This
marriage is the subject of my ardent prayer; therefore
it is well, it is right. I know the Lord hears His poor
ungrateful servant, and this completely satisfies me as to
the result.

"*Rosshdu, April 26*. — My beloved H. and Mr R.
are now in London. They have been peculiarly on my
mind to-day, and I have again and again prayed impor-
tunately for them. I rejoice in this; for I know that

prayer, real prayer, is heard; and, therefore, I believe that spiritual and eternal blessings await my children. I am happy to add that since my return home I have felt spiritually minded, which is life and peace. I feel confidence in God, and commit all my concerns into His hand, believing that He will manage for me, what might seem immaterial to a fellow-worm, but which is not beneath the notice of the Eternal. I expect to have more tokens of His faithfulness yet to write of.

"*Edinburgh, March 20*, 1831. — I feel that I am not living for God solely and exclusively, as I ought to do, and as His people do. I feel a worldly, carnal spirit, and a sort of *put-off* religion which quiets the conscience, but which does me little good, and is not the radical principle influencing every thought. I know it is worldly care which has hurt me, and that Satan has found out a point in which I am indeed vulnerable, my anxiety respecting my family; and he tempts me to forsake the fountain of living water and hew out broken cisterns, which can hold no water.

"*Rosshdu, June 12*. — Another happy Sabbath spent at home. This being Bonhill sacrament there is no sermon at Luss. The influences of the Spirit were certainly visible this day in leading my heart to God. The character of Christ appeared to me in *something* of its genuine loveliness. I could pray with fervor, and feel what I read. Dr Hamilton's 'Mourner in Zion Comforted', I found in many parts in unison with my own experience, and I read it with pleasure. Thus, when God is pleased to breathe on these dry bones, they live. It may be needless to repeat that I am nothing, and can do nothing, but I am deeply sensible of the truth of it. My family having grown up, their various interests, and connexions, and plans have certainly led me in heart more into the

world than I ever expected to be; but the Lord is faithful!
He will find a method of escape, and surely I shall enter
glory, shouting, '*Grace, grace*'.

"*Regency-square, Brighton, Nov. 27.* — Last Lord's-day
was little like the Sabbath to me.   I was in the steam-
vessel, and unable to sit up at all from sickness. But in
my little berth I remembered my God, and was enabled
to confide in Him. Some repairs necessary to the safety
of the ship, which had encountered a storm in coming
from London, rendered a delay of two days necessary,
and thus I was compelled to be at sea on Sunday, which
I had particularly planned to avoid. Our passage was
perfectly safe, and my prayers respecting it all heard.
Was one day in London. How affecting to see that place!
so many interesting years have elapsed since I was there
before, and two of my dearest friends there, my much-
loved sister and excellent nurse, Morris, are gone to
glory. On my way here I saw Mr Maitland, of Clapham,
— Oh! how changed! He is quite helpless from palsy,
but he is one of the Lord's people, and all is well. Nothing
could be better ordered than every thing has been respecting this journey. Sarah and James have accompanied
me, and Sir James is to follow in January. Mr Reade*
and Helen we found well, and they are to be with us
here. The Lord has fixed the bounds of our habitation
in a good and cheerful house, and to crown all, my heart
has been much with Him in prayer and praise. Went to
St. James's, and heard an excellent sermon. — 'The name
of the Lord is a strong tower'. What a tower of strength
that name has been to me! And shall it not continue to
be so till death, in judgment, and throughout eternity?

"*Jan. 1*, 1832. — Have again been twice at church,
first in the Chapel Royal, where I saw their Majesties,

* John Page Reade, Esq., of Stutton, Suffolk, her son-in-law.

and heard the Bishop of ———— preach. I trust the truths of the Gospel may sometimes bless the Royal party, but certainly it was not so to-day. I felt interested in our Queen, who seems religiously inclined.

"*Jan. 15.* — Have again listened with much pleasure twice to Mr Elliott. Sir James arrived here in perfect safety last week, and my brother George is also with us. He gave a noble proof to-day of devotedness to the King of kings. When an invitation from the palace came for him to dine with our monarch on this sacred day, he did not hesitate a moment to send a refusal, which he did in most respectful and affectionate terms. How this will be taken it is impossible to say; but I rejoice that an opportunity has been afforded my brother of shewing his sincerity at the Court, and that I have a brother capable of acting thus. May the Almighty bless and preserve him!"

The incident to which the foregoing extract relates afforded great delight to Lady Colquhoun. Her brother was staying with her at the time, and as valued relics she preserved the card of invitation, dated, "Pavilion, Jan. 15, 1832", and a copy of the answer, which she sought leave to transcribe. And we are sure that Sir George Sinclair will forgive the publication of that letter if it contribute, however remotely, to a cause which he has much at heart.

"**Sire,**— **No one can** value more highly than I do the honor and privilege of being at any time permitted to enjoy that social intercourse with which your Majesty has, on so many occasions, been pleased to indulge me for so many years. But I am fully aware with how much consideration your Majesty enters into the feelings and sympathizes with the wishes of those whom you honor with your friendship. I have for some time past been led to entertain very different notions from those which I once cherished as to the observance of this day, and subscribe fully to the views which the Church, and I may add, the Legislature, have laid down with respect to its importance. Encouraged by the latitude of discussion which your Majesty has so long and so kindly vouchsafed, I lately took the liberty, though in opposition to your Majesty's opinion, to maintain that not merely a *part* but the *whole* of this day should be devoted to those great purposes for which divine authority has set it apart. I may be permitted to add, from grateful experience, that this decision has its reward even here. I have found that God honors those who honor Him, and though encompassed with sin and infirmity, I can testify, that He is not an austere Master, that He has strength for all our weaknesses, indemnity for all our sacrifices, and consolation for all our troubles.

"I feel bound, on principle of conscience, to deny myself, what is always one of my most valued gratifications, that of paying my humble and most affectionate respects this day, and must rest satisfied with renewing in my retirement those earnest supplications for your Majesty's health and happiness which are equally dictated by regard for the public welfare and by a thankfully cherished remembrance of much distinguished and unmerited kindness.

" I have the honor," &c.

The sequel was no less worthy of the King. Next morning, whilst they were seated round the breakfast table, a royal messenger arrived charged with an invitation to the Pavilion that evening. His Majesty made no allusion to the letter; but to show how perfectly he appreciated the motives of his guest, he went beyond even his usual urbanity and kindness; and to the close of his reign no interruption occurred in a friendship equally honourable to the accomplished commoner and to the frank and warm-hearted monarch — a circumstance to which Lady Colquhoun refers in the Journal of the following Sabbath :—

"The manner in which my dear brother acted last Lord's-day turned out well, and much to the credit of the King, who asked him to dinner on Monday, and paid him marked attention. Thus, 'them that honor Him, God will honor.'"

To every pious subject it must also be a source of lively satisfaction to know that in the Pavilion itself originated measures which have materially tended to promote the better observance of the Sabbath in Brighton. It is said that there were certain arrangements in the Royal household which undesignedly entailed a large amount of Sunday labor; but when the facts were represented to Queen Adelaide, she immediately commanded that the orders in question should be given on Monday instead of Saturday as heretofore; and this act of Christian consideration has been extensively copied, to the great relief of many a laundress who formerly could not "remember the Sabbath-day to keep it holy". In unison with this tribute to the divine command was the injunction of our present Queen, forbidding the exhibition, on the Lord's-day, of the state-apartments at Windsor Castle; an act which, along with Her Majesty's patronage of the Sabbath-observance movement among the working classes, has given a much-loved Sovereign an additional claim to the gratitude and attachment of a Christian people.

And here we may notice the loyalty of Lady Colquhoun's religion. She had no ambition to "dwell in kings' houses", and notwithstanding the favor in which both her father and brother stood with successive sovereigns, her biographer is not sure that she was ever presented at Court. And when on the occasion of the Royal visit to Edinburgh in 1822, her husband went to do homage to George IV., from aversion to scenes of gaiety and grandeur she forbore to accompany him. But frequent allusions in her diary show how eagerly she hailed every indication of piety in high places, and how mindful she was to make intercession for kings and all in authority. She had links of attachment to the throne which gave to her loyalty a sentiment more affectionate than the duteous feeling of an ordinary subject; and it would be well for the land if the same personal and prayerful interest in its rulers were shared by a larger portion of the religious community.

"*London, March 25*, 1832. — We returned here last night, after spending a few days pleasantly at Mr Fuller Maitland's. We are on our way to Stutton, where we intend being to-morrow. At Kingston I went with Miss Massie and saw my beloved sister's grave; it is in a pretty and peaceful resting-place. The chancel of the church where she is laid is venerable and very spacious; there she will arise at the resurrection of the just. I have felt animated and invigorated by intercourse with the pious. Oh for grace to follow the footsteps of the flock! To-day I again had the privilege of hearing Mr Howells, and having a pencil I wrote down a few of his striking observations. From the first lesson for the day (Gen. xxxix.) he noticed the superiority which God's people may acquire over temptation; that our best security from it is in flight; that the reality of our principles is generally in some way or other *tried;* and that we may learn from this chapter tenderness to delinquents, which Potiphar showed to Joseph, believing him guilty. The second lesson was in John xii.; from which he observed that our Lord's humiliation was real, and not like man's, who is often proud of it; that Christ's death was as necessary for our salvation as that wheat must be put into the ground before it springs again; that the beauty of God is holiness, and how can we hope to attain beauty in anything else? The sermon was from Jeremiah xxxii. 40. He said, God puts His fear in the heart and keeps it there. The will of God is all holy and good, and when we shall know all His counsel we shall rejoice in it for ever. The fear is in the believer's heart; his whole heart is changed to love what God loves. He has motives to fear and love God that angels have not. They were not redeemed from sin and saved by Christ's death as he is. Believers fear God from His moral perfections. They fear Him in His providence. Have we then seen the beauty of God in His holiness? Have we experienced the pleasure of religion? And do we rejoice in the appointments of God? He concluded thus : God appoints everything for *me*; I know it is best for me; I have nothing to do with it, but rest satisfied with His will. Everything is welcome that God wills. I shall rejoice in it hereafter, and I *will* rejoice in it *now*. I have no anxiety, for all is arranged by infinite wisdom, and by my Father.

"*Rosshdu, June 10*, 1832. — There is again no sermon in this parish, and again I am spending the day happily and profitably. Enjoyed much trust and confidence in prayer. Read over a year or two of this book — the latter part of it; and with thankfulness and pleasure I trace that religion has advanced during the last twelve months. before this there was a season of declension. I know well by whose power the good seed is preserved; and I thank

God and take courage. I was much gratified to observe more attention to religious reading in my family than common. I went out with the Bible and read at the side of the lake, with much pleasure, the last chapter of St. Luke. I have also satisfaction in the instruction of my maids, who were all attentive and interested.

"*Sept.* 16, 1832. — I hope I continue in a frame of mind more like a Christian, than I sometimes experience, but I am far from meaning that any high degree of devotional feeling is my attainment. My best days are thus spent; in prayer I feel that I address an exalted Friend, who, I believe, listens to and answers my supplications. I feel a greater sense of the reality of the being and presence of God. I go from prayer, like Hannah, 'with my countenance no more sad.' I feel a greater solicitude that myself and others should do the will of God. I feel a greater satisfaction in thinking of God and a future state, and I am more reconciled to the thoughts of leaving the world. And then all seems bright and cheering, for I commit my present and future concerns to the guidance of Almighty power and wisdom. Such as this, is the most I know of experimental religion; ecstasies or any rapturous emotions were never mine. Perfect, Lord, that which concerneth me!

"*Leamington, Royal Hotel, March 3*, 1833. — I have been here more than a week, and have reason to bless God for many things regarding my removal from home and the state of health in which I found my dear H—. We are comfortably settled here, and I commit my way to the Lord, trusting in Him. My religious feeling has been very low of late, but seems to revive in some degree to-day. I have not been able to attend public worship, having caught a bad cold on the journey.

"*March 17.* — I certainly have to lament (yet how little,

in truth, do I feel it!) that religion is at a very low ebb
with me at present. I have been twice at church to-day,
and in the morning heard a scriptural sermon from Mr
Pope; but I have little feeling of the truths of the Gospel.
In the evening I had the chambermaids of the Hotel up,
as I had last Lord's-day, to read and explain to them from
the Bible, and I was interested and did my best to make
the way of salvation plain to them. I have also been distributing tracts here."

It would be a disastrous winter which should surprise
us in midsummer; but the great Creator has a way of
bringing it so gently on that the world is ready for its
arrival, and all the better for its visit. The day shortens;
the forest seres; and the world is warned. The air cools;
the fervors of the solstice are forgotten, and before the
frost appears the world is acclimatized. And by a process
somewhat similar, when grief is coming our Heavenly
Father often forewarns and fortifies His children. So was
it with the subject of this biography. In her serene and
happy domestic life the summer was now past and the
harvest ending; but God forewarned her. She saw with
steps progressive, though not startling, that disease advancing which was to summon from beside her the husband of her youth; and the impression of approaching
widowhood was strengthened by a dream which so
fastened in her memory that she could not shake it out.
But she had a still better preparation. There is no fence
against the storm so effectual as vigorous health and a
pulse firmly bounding; and God gave her the preparation
of soul-prosperity. The last quotation from her journal
complains of languor; the next extracts will show how
delectation and trust in God revived, and how by bene-
ficient labors she was regaining spiritual tone and elas-
ticity. Nor, in connexion with the sequel, will the reader

fail to observe that special Providence which called her attention so seasonably to the treatise of the good old Puritan.

"*Rossdhu, April 28.* — When thinking over the ways of Providence, I saw in a bookseller's shop Flavel's 'Divine Conduct of Providence'. Struck with the title I bought it. Every word came home to my heart and to my experience. Oh let me praise the Lord for wonderful compassion to a poor sinful worm! I feel safe in His everlasting arms, and in believing that He will perform all things for me.

"*May 5.* — To-day I am at home, having a cold, or probably influenza, which is all over the kingdom at present. I bless God that my frame of mind, although not particularly lively in religious duty, is settled, calm, and not without interest in the subject. I have been enabled to pray in reality and to commit every concern to God, and to view Him ordering all my little affairs as if there were no other being to care for in the universe. It is thus only that we can bring it home to our hearts that the great God careth for *us*; for we are apt to imagine that, like man, He cannot manage so much at once, and will be forgetful of what is infinitely interesting to His creatures. Flavel's book on Providence continues to charm me, being completely in unison with all my experience. All that he says I have known and felt.

"*June 2.* — Since writing the above I have been in Edinburgh, with Sir James. His medical attendant there (Dr Wood) has prescribed various remedies, but evidently thinks seriously of his complaints. O Lord, fit and prepare him and me for whatever may be Thy will respecting him. I feel assured that God is ordering everything for the very best as regards him; and one thing gives me the greatest pleasure — the religious impressions my dear husband seems to feel.

"*July 30.* — I was at church and taught the school. Oh! for ever blessed be the Lord! I now feel as if on a rock, as if God will assuredly so manage every concern for good that no evil shall ever befal me. I do commit my way to Him and trust also in Him. The children whom I teach at the school appear interested, and I am encouraged to hope for a spiritual blessing to them. Amen.

"*Oct. 27.* — To-day I took leave of the Sabbath-school, the days being too short to admit of teaching it. I spoke to the girls as impressively as I could, and was happy to observe the greatest interest in most of them. The regular scholars, after a short vacation, will meet for religious instruction on Mondays. I rejoiced this Sabbath in the Lord, who performeth all things for me, and in whom I am complete. Nothing beside Him have I to trust to for temporal or spiritual benefits — yet what more would I desire than a *Divine Redeemer?*

"*Jan. 12,* 1834. — Have heard of the death of my dear Christian sister-in-law, Mrs Campbell, of Stonefield. She died at Pau, full of peace and hope. She will be an irreparable loss to her family, and a real loss to me. May I be enabled to follow her steps, for they lead to glory.

"*Edinburgh, April 6.* — Was much gratified last week by finding that my little work, 'Impressions of the Heart', is completely sold off and out of print, and that another edition is called for. To me it is a very pleasing thought that it is now in the hands of so many. I feel a hope that the Lord will use me for His glory. I thank God and take courage in the prosecution of the work I am now writing. Neither will be published till next winter, as this town will soon empty now.

"*Rossdhu, April 20.* — Once more settled in our beauti-ful abode, where nature, or rather nature's God, has done so much to charm the eye. I have much reason for

gratitude that my dear husband has been so much benefited by medical advice while in Edinburgh. We have all
returned in prosperous circumstances; but I am detained
at home to-day by a rheumatic pain in the face, which has
been troublesome for more than a week. This forenoon
it is easier; and, along with the Bible, I have been reading
Neff's interesting 'Memoir.' Have felt rather stupid and
sleepy; but our merciful High Priest is touched with a
feeling of our infirmities.

"*May 18.* — I was enlivened in religious respects last
week by a visit, for a single night, from good Dr Malan,
of Geneva. It is now eight years since he was here before;
and although I was not so much impressed by his conversation as I then was, still I think I was sensibly benefited by it. I am led at present to live nearer to God,
with a more simple dependance upon Him for everything.
This day I was more spiritually minded than last Sabbath,
and employed myself as usual.

"*Dec. 7.* — Experienced real joy this morning in considering that some works of mercy I lately performed are
acceptable and pleasing to God. This was no self-righteous
feeling; for I well know with how much sin all I do is
mingled; but it was delight in thinking I had pleased my
best Friend. I continue happy in communion with Him,
and trusting in His grace.

"*May 3*, 1835. — My kind Christian friend, Dr Hamilton, of Strathblane, is, alas! no more. He died, after a
short illness, a fortnight ago. Last week I paid my first
visit to the prison at Dumbarton. I have undertaken to
superintend the female prisoners. May a blessing rest on
my poor endeavours!"

It was by the excellent Mrs Fry that Lady Colquhoun
was first enlisted in the arduous business of prison-
visitation. In a letter written to Mrs Reade, about this

period, she alludes to these labors :—

"I was very much interested in the poor depraved boy, and have succeeded in obtaining permission to have him taught to read, about which I was very anxious, as in this way access would be got to his mind. And much to my gratification I have got a very fit person to teach him. He is a schoolmaster in the place, and enters zealously into the business. He went to see his scholar when I was there, and said he had never met with such deplorable ignorance. The youth had never seen a Bible, had never heard of a God, excepting to hear His name taken in vain, and had never entered a church. His master is to strive to instruct him in religion along with the A, B, C. I also visited the poor woman the day before she was liberated. She received me with great pleasure, said she 'had been *through* the book I gave her, three times,' and expressed much gratitude for some tracts I left with her. I asked if she would read them. 'Yes, ma'am, that I will,' said she, 'and take them wi' me wherever I go.' She is poor, and after thinking whether I ought to give her money or not, as she is rather too *covetous*! I ventured to give her half-a-crown, thinking she might have nothing when she left the prison. This quite overcame her, and she only said, 'Ma'am, I *do not* deserve it,' with tears in her eyes."

"*July 12.* — I have seen much since last I wrote here," the journal resumes, "having been with Sir James and Sarah in Ireland. I spent two Sabbaths very happily there — the first in Dublin, where I heard Mr Matthias, of Bethesda Chapel, preach, and Mr Stewart, of Union Chapel, both dear servants of God. The sermon of the latter, on the influences of the Spirit, came home to my heart; and the whole service, which was in the Presbyterian form, seemed to do me good. The next Sabbath we were at Cushendall, on our way to the Giant's Cause-

way — a sweet little village, and where there is a Gospel
ministry. I enjoyed the whole day, and my heart seemed
alive and happy. I distributed some tracts in poor Ireland,
which were gladly received, even by the Catholics. On
our return to Belfast, I was gratified to meet some
apparently very serious Christians, in a shop of the name
of M'——. One of the sisters gave me a phial of their
lavender water as a remembrance.

"*Sept. 13.* — Have been in Edinburgh, where my dear
husband's health called me. He consulted Dr Abercrombie
and Dr Wood. The opinion of both seems to be, that his
complaints are alarming. I have long thought so. Oh!
may the Almighty fit him for death, if such is His will,
and give me strength of body and mind for whatever
scenes await me.

"*Sept. 20.* — My dear Sir James having been worse
than usual, we have fixed on going to Edinburgh to reside
on Tuesday next. This is, therefore, my last Sabbath here
for the present; and, alas! it appears to me probable that
the term when I inhabited this retired and beautiful abode
is now about to end. If so, the Almighty will again fix
the bounds of my habitation, and I shall be where it is
best I should. I have endeavoured to call my beloved
husband's attention to what I conceive to be his real
state, and I have the heartfelt satisfaction to see him
anxious to prepare for life or death. To-day I remained
at home with him. Everything regarding our removal to
Edinburgh seems providentially arranged. My God continues good.

"*110 Princes-street, Edinburgh, Sept. 27.* — We have
been here for some days, and all has been mercifully
ordered respecting our removal. My dear husband is, on
the whole, better, and has been able to-day to attend in
a small chapel in Young-street, where we have got seats,

and where a truly pious young man, of the name of
Moody, preaches. I have felt rather enlivened from his
preaching and prayers, for I have been dull and dead in
a great measure to spiritual things. One thought has
cheered me — that it appears to me I could give up
everything here for God, were I called to it, and did I
see Him as He is. I think I shall soon require all the
consolation the Gospel affords, and I shall not need
without enjoying it. He who has brought me hitherto,
and supported me in every emergency, will continue to
do so to the end.

"*Sunday, Nov. 1.* — Since writing here this day fortnight, there is no very material change in my dear charge.
I am still passing through the dark scene of my nearest
earthly relation's death, or rather its forerunners. He has
talked to me frequently of his religious hopes. He lies like
a little child at the foot of the cross. He says he is willing
to be saved in Christ's own way, and to serve God to all
eternity, and to cast his crown at the foot of the Lamb,
as humbly as any in heaven. I have always prayed, at
least to see him *die* in the Lord, and trust my merciful,
forgiving Saviour has received him into the number of
His own. This is the sacrament Sabbath here. I am unable
to leave Sir James long, but mean to attend a table
service in St. George's, and perhaps the evening sermon.

"*8th.* — I am now at the 'post of observation, darker
every hour.' Since last Sabbath my beloved husband has
visibly declined. To-day and yesterday he has spent in
bed, and I have been unable to leave him to attend the
house of God. He enters on no subject of conversation
now. The only one that seems to interest him is religion,
and he will lift his hand in supplication when I have
finished praying with him.

"*15th.* — Still my nearest earthly relative lives, and is

better in body than last Sabbath. I read to him a few
verses of the Bible from time to time, to which he listens
with interest. He sat up several times to-day. I was able
to attend Mr Moody's chapel in the afternoon. I feel
safe in Almighty care and protection. My temporal
mercies overflow. I have everything I can want for
myself and Sir James; and I trust that every step regarding us both is ordered for good.

"*Jan. 3,* 1836. — This new year has come mournfully
in to me — my father just dead, my husband without
hope of recovery! But still the Lord liveth! Blessed, said
the Psalmist, be my Rock! God is indeed a Refuge from
the storm. O that I could lean more on a Foundation so
sure! There is no risk that it will totter, or fail me.

"*24th.* — Still my dear Sir James lives. He is the
shadow of what he was. His medical attendants give me
no hope that he will long survive. Perhaps ere this
hallowed day returns, he may be gone to the house
appointed for all living, and his spirit may be rejoicing
among the blessed. I wait the sovereign will of my Lord,
and believe that He is doing well. Last night, in reading
a sermon of my late worthy pastor, Dr Buchanan, I was
reminded of his practical piety; and the beauty of the
Gospel precepts captivated me. I remembered former
days, when the purity of the lessons of God's Word was
so much my delight. I felt as if I had lost ground, and
earnestly prayed to grow and shine in universal holiness."

Mournfully passed that long winter; nor were their
toils who watched over the sufferer cheered by any hope
of recovery. And to affection it made the trial greater
that the mental faculties at last partook of the body's
extreme exhaustion, and left little power of intercourse.
But to Lady Colquhoun it was a ceaseless comfort, and
it helped to inspire her fervent prayers, that up to the

last hour of consciousness her beloved husband listened
with meek earnestness to every portion of Scripture which
she read, and joined devoutly in every petition offered in
his hearing; whilst in prospect of his coming change, he
uniformly declared that the Saviour was his only hope.
During these silent watchings, word was brought that
her venerable father was laid aside from his long and
patriotic labors; and, throughout his brief decline, Sir
James found a melancholy source of interest in the communications which daily went and came betwixt their
sick-rooms.

On the 21st of December Lady Colquhoun spent some
time with her father, and in the course of conversation
he expressed a wish that she would affix her name to her
publications. Two hours afterwards the tidings of his
death gave touching import to the interview, and added
to the request the solemnity of a dying charge. Sir John
was gathered to his fathers from the midst of a hale old
age and its cheerful occupations; and in a few weeks
some of the mourners who encircled his grave in Holyrood
Chapel were called to join the sable procession which,
up the Vale of Leven, and through the solemnized
hamlets, conveyed to the ancestral cemetery the dust of
his son-in-law. As it passed, one aged clansman was
propped up in bed, and when he saw the hearse containing the lifeless form of his much-loved landlord, the old
man fainted away; and everywhere was manifested the
emotion of a people reverential to old lineage, and grateful to the proprietor whom constant residence had
converted into their friend and protector. It was a fine
winter's day, and the sunshine had suspended the frost,
when, round the old "chapel," were congregated the
tenantry of Luss, Row, and Arrochar, as well as many
friends, and the gentlemen of the county, and, borne on

the shoulders of three Grants and three Colquhouns, the coffin was lowered into its appropriate resting-place.* Soon after, the sanctuary where so many generations sleep was set in order, and in its roofless solitude, or beneath the shadow of its coeval evergreens, the widowed survivor often lingered; and there she often mused on the day when, in the rising of His redeemed, the Saviour shall complete His own resurrection, and consummate their felicity.

The following is the passage in the journal which records this most solemn occurrence in her personal history:—

"*Feb. 7*, 1836. — At length my fears are realized! He to whom I was related by the nearest earthly tie, departed this life on Wednesday, the 3rd, and has left me to mourn his loss. I was indeed long prepared for the blow; yet nature will feel, nor are we forbidden to weep. I dread being more sensible to the affliction hereafter, as there is a bustle incident to such a time which has a tendency to divert the mind, and, alas! to rob us of the improvement we might derive from it. Apparently my beloved husband suffered for fourteen hours before rather severely; but his medical attendants assured me that from want of consciousness he was not sensible of pain. Yesterday the dear remains were deposited in the coffin; I loved to look at them, and feel grieved that they must be removed from my care. The key of the room I kept, and many times I had looked on the countenance, which

---

* Sir John Sinclair died Dec. 21, 1835, aged eighty-one. Sir James Colquhoun died Feb. 3, 1836, aged sixty-one. The usage above mentioned has obtained since the time of Sir James Grant. He married Anne Colquhoun, heiress of Luss. Their eldest son succeeded to the Grant estate, and was an ancestor of the Earl of Seafield; their second son succeeded to the estate and baronetage of Colquhoun.

fully retained the likeness, and was placid and serene.
O Lord, I would trust that he is justified freely by Thy
grace, that he is accepted without money and without
price. This was all his hope and all his desire. And now
be to me a husband, a father, a sanctifier, a strong tower
to which I may continually resort. All my hope centres
in Thee, my God, my all!"

It was during this sad and anxious winter that the new
edition of her "Impressions" was published, as well as a
companion-volume, entitled "The Kingdom of God." In
obedience to both her father and husband she now overcame her ratural sensitiveness and placed her name on
the title-page; and there can be no doubt that this
authentication added weight and interest to works which
the religious community had already learned to appreciate.
How little of literary vanity mingled with what was truly
a Christian sacrifice may be seen from the following
extract:—

"*Jan. 10,* 1836. — Last week I did what I never
expected to do. I gave my name to the public as the
authoress of my books! Not two hours before he died,
my father requested that I should do so, and my dear
husband always wished it; so that, from concurring
circumstances, I have thought it the will of God. And
now, O my God! for thy honor and the good of men
I have made some sacrifice; therefore in mercy use my
works to promote these glorious purposes."

Amidst many communications received from sympathizing friends during that sorrowful spring, none was
more welcome than the letter of her true-hearted correspondent in Canada, Mrs Charles Scott. It is dated
from the "Cottage of the Falls, U. C., April 25, 1836:—

"Need I tell you with what deep interest I read your
letter from Edinburgh, my very dear Lady Colquhoun.

It was long on the way, but the sight of your hand-
writing gladdened my heart in this distant land, when
it did arrive. It tells me of affliction, of the Lord's hand
being at work, but shows me, at the same time, a mind
resting on the Rock of Ages, a heart supported by the
everlasting arms, and much, very much sweetness mingled
in the cup administered by the hand of Love. I cannot
tell you, dear Lady C., how much I long for further
accounts of you. Your venerable father's death I had
seen an account of in the newspapers. But your threat-
ened affliction in Sir James's illness I had not heard of,
and do not now know if it may have pleased our Lord
to give an unexpected turn to his illness, or if you are
a 'widow indeed.' If such is the case, I have not the
slightest doubt that you continue to find our faithful
God very present with you, leading you to experience
the fulness of many promises, which before you read and
believed, but had no opportunity experimentally to prove.
He who has been precious to you, and present with you
so long, who gave you quietness of soul in the midst of
outward trouble, will, I doubt not, continue unceasingly
so to the end. This I know, but yet I long much to hear
particulars from yourself. What a strong foundation the
Christian stands upon, for time, as well as for eternity!
God in Christ includes all that can be desired; and
though our sins may appear deeper and darker each
year that passes over, yet it does not seem to depress,
but to raise the heart in increased thankfulness to Him
who pardons them all, who 'blots out, as a thick cloud,
our transgressions, and as a cloud our sins.' . . . . This
situation, so far as temporal matters are concerned, is
most desirable for a summer residence. Nothing can
exceed the grandeur of the Falls, and no pen could give
the least idea of them. We are within about ten minutes'

walk of the upper bank, and the view from this cottage is very beautiful: the rapids of the Niagara river just above the Falls, dashing on in continued foam, till lost in the dense body of spray, generally ascending from the Falls. The winter has been the most severe experienced for twenty years, the thermometer varying from zero to 16° below it. Extremely unpleasant such cold is to the feeling, but it has pleased God to continue us all in good health."

CHAPTER V.

Forgetting those things which are behind, and reaching forth unto those things which are before, I press toward the mark for the prize of the high calling of God in Christ Jesus.

— Philippians iii. 13, 14.

Since the dear hour that brought me to thy foot,
And cut up all my follies by the root,
I never trusted in an arm but thine,
Nor hoped but in thy righteousness divine.
My prayers and alms,—
Forgive their evil, and accept their good;
I cast them at thy feet — my only plea
Is what it was, dependance upon thee :
While struggling in the vale of tears below,
That never fail'd, nor shall it fail me now.

Cowper's "Truth".

GENTLY as Lady Colquhoun woke up to her bereavement, and notwithstanding the redoubled assiduities of an affectionate family, the desolate reality sometimes overpowered her; and, though still able to regard it as her home, her return to Rossdhu next spring revived in all its anguish the woeful consciousness of widowhood. And it was many a day before the bright landscape shone again through that thick crape in which grief had veiled it. Long afterwards we find her recording — "I feel the loss of my very dear husband's society more than I did shortly after his death. To me there is an inexpressible blank in this house, and I would gladly leave it. However, I ought to be thankful for the many mercies which still surround me, and should cast my care on my covenant God, believing that He does right." Nor did her covenant God forsake her. Mournfully released from her long ministrations in the sick-room, and no longer called to discharge those multifarious duties which he had so thoroughly and gracefully fulfilled, "her Maker was her husband," and she gave herself to the Lord's work with new consecration. In Sept. of that year she writes to her married daughter:—

"I should have particularly liked to be more alone when Mr Moody was here; but who knows but a blessing might be sent to others through his visit? He came very opportunely to help me about my favorite plan — the chapel at Helensburgh. Mr M. got quite interested in the subject, and in Glasgow went to different influential clergymen to state the matter to them. They said, so liberal a proposal should never be rejected, though it were only to set an example to other landed proprietors; and one said that for a long time he had heard of nothing which gave him so great pleasure. So I trust yet to make it out. Another church also interests me much at present. One of James's, in Caithness (W——n), has become vacant. The son of the late incumbent seems so very superior a young man, that however much I am opposed to this 'hereditary succession,' I think he will be the minister. J. appears to leave it entirely to me to decide, and, thanks be to God for so great a blessing, as the power of placing in this parish a devoted pastor. This is a long story about churches; but, oh, dear H., my heart is full of the subject. The interest I feel in religion deepens, and fain would I impart somewhat of it to those who are dear to me. I feel that the time to improve for this purpose is short; that 'the night cometh when no man can work;' and earnestly do I pray that my H. may be brought to the foot of the cross, there to seek and to find that satisfaction of spirit which she *will* find in nothing else."

Helensburgh is a much-frequented watering-place on the estuary of the Clyde, and within the Luss estate; and the scheme for providing it with a chapel of its own was the first of several Church-extension movements to which Lady Colquhoun largely contributed. The chapel of her Edinburgh pastor, Mr Moody, was another, and though these erections were soon forfeited to a very different ministry from that which the pious donors contemplated —nowise disheartened, with the new emergency she redoubled her munificence; and after this she was so impressed with the spiritual destitution of overgrown towns and manufacturing villages, that it became a ruling object in her life to provide more Christian teachers and more sanctuaries. Like the father of church-builders,* she could not 'give sleep to her eyes,' till she 'found out habitations for the mighty God;' and, like the projector of the temple, her devout intentions and self-denying gifts were requited with soul-prosperity.

In her Sabbath-school she now formed an adult class, and adopted a system, which she thus announces to Mrs Reade:—

"I have begun a new plan at our school on Sundays —a class for grown-up girls. They commit nothing to memory, but I explain the Bible and Catechism. I adopted it in consequence of seeing Mr Moody's on Monday evenings. The class is flourishing and always increasing. Several old people attend regularly, and I hope to have more. My own maids also asked leave to go; so, with the children, I have a pretty large congre-

* Psalm cxxxii.

gation, and it needs some *nerve*. But I hope to be enabled to go on, and I hear it is much liked. May God send a blessing!"

These "Horæ Sabbaticæ" were not only very popular, but became extremely useful. During the week, her Ladyship studied with much care the passage which she intended to explain, and exerted herself in finding anecdotes and illustrations which might render it more interesting and memorable. Her manner was full of calm benevolence and mild persuasion; and whatever nervousness she might feel, her address was so fluent, natural, and dignified, that the thoughts of the audience were solely directed to the subject. In unison with that devout and holy life which they all knew that their kind instructor led, these exhortations were singularly impressive. On a dying bed more than one of her young hearers gave evidence of having been by this means brought to the Saviour; and from the grateful tenderness in which many of the survivors hold their teacher's memory it may be hoped that all her "works" have not yet "followed" her. It is to these Sabbath-evening exercises that the following entries in her journal refer:—

"*Rossdhu, July 30*, 1837. — My Sabbaths are now much occupied in preparing to address my class, which I do at some length. Every week it has increased, and though we had two additional benches today, there was scarcely room enough for them. I am much encouraged, and this morning prayed so earnestly for a blessing, that I feel confident it shall be given. Earnest prayer is a gift, and is bestowed when God designs to hear. I always feel fagged in the evening afterwards, and can do little.

"*August 6*. — Being Arrochar sacrament, no sermon at Luss. I was, as usual, occupied with the school. There were fewer this evening, as many of them had gone to

Arrochar. My God was present in prayer at night. Last week my son James was elected Member for the county. John and his family leave us to-morrow.

"*Sept. 3.* — Have little to say to-day but that I was much gratified by a very large attendance at the school. There was scarcely room for any more, and there must have been about sixty present. I likewise observe with great pleasure the appearance of interest in some who attend; in one or two I think I can scarcely be mistaken. Have been much assisted in preparation for my class, and, at the time, in speaking to them and in prayer. To-night feel inspirited, yet cannot say that devotional feeling is strong.

"*17.* — Lady Sinclair, and Diana and Catherine are here. They went with me to the school and appeared much pleased. The children proved a number of doctrines very well.

"*Oct. 8.* — Have prayed very earnestly to-day, and with great pleasure have read the 'Life of Brainerd'. At the school had a good attendance. Went to bed joyful, the words, 'He that believeth on the Son hath everlasting life,' being delightfully impressed on my mind. The freeness of redemption and the simplicity of believing came to me with clearness, so that I could not but say, I *do* believe, I *have* everlasting life.

"*15.* — Penitence was in exercise this morning. It was the last day of my class, which I have been enabled to continue for four months without a Sabbath's intermission. Now it darkens too soon after church to admit of its being kept up any longer. A great many were present. I felt affected in speaking to them, and thought they appeared so too. Lord, bless this attempt to save souls and glorify thy name! It is a pleasure to me to think it has been made, and God has wonderfully assisted me."

Should any one be moved by this example to make an effort in his own locality, he may find instruction in her Ladyship's procedure, as well as an incentive in her Ladyship's success. Allowing something for the rank, and something more for the talent of the teacher, her usefulness was mainly owing to her affection, her prayerfulness, her diligence, and her hopefulness. She loved her humble neighbours, and instead of coming forth to dispense a weekly lecture or reproof, she re-appeared amongst them from week to week, with the law of kindness on her lips and cordiality in every feature, and in each earnest statement and solemn entreaty they recognised their friend and well-wisher. But before she came to them she had been to God, and upon her labor of love she had implored her Heavenly Father's blessing. And, then, to show that her prayers were sincere and sanguine, she grudged no labor, and she betrayed no gloom. Her assiduous preparation, and her cheerful, encouraging address, were the natural sequel to fervent and believing petitions. "In testimony of desire and assurance to be heard, she had said, Amen:"* but she not only said it in the closet, she lived it throughout the day. Her diligent study of the subject was a prolonged Amen in the ear of God, and showed how desirous was her prayer; her radiant and expectant look was to her little congregation a visible Amen, and told them how assured she was that God had heard her, and how hopeful she was that God had mercy in reserve for them. And we know no other path to eminent usefulness, except like perseverance in affectionate industry and hopeful prayer. Perhaps, dear reader, you are disappointed by some previous failure. Once on a time you gathered a

* "Shorter Catechism", Q. 107.

few poor people, or an adult class, into a cottage or the
servants' hall; but it was with difficulty you filled up the
hour, and next evening, instead of a doubled attendance,
only nine of the dozen returned; and instead of multi-
plying to fifty or sixty, as in the present case, in six
weeks the last straggler had stolen away. Nor can you
blame yourself; for your motive was good, and you
prayed for a blessing. True; but allow us respectfully to
ask, What was your style of address? Was it kind and
endearing? or was it not rather magisterial, perceptive,
reprimanding? The eloquence which at once wins and
commands unlettered hearers, is like His whom "the
common people heard so gladly," — it is the sympathetic
effusion of a superior nature; the utterance of a mind
so elevated that it need take no thought for its own dignity,
but withal so cordial and compassionate, that it creates
or catches emotion in every countenance it looks upon.
The Cottage Readings of Lady Colquhoun possessed this
double charm: her hearers could never forget the
Christian lady, and she never forgot her fellow-sinners
and fellow-candidates for an immortal crown; so that a
sweet benignity pervaded her exhortations and remonstrances and her gentleness was full of "authority."
And did you make your hearers feel not only that you
wished them well, but that you were full of hope regarding them? Lady Colquhoun knew that the Gospel is the
"power of God unto salvation," and she announced it
with a joyful confidence; and although the listlessness
of her servants or scholars might send an occasional pang
through her spirit, it never tinged her words with resent-
ment; but, in the exercise of that love which "hopeth all
things," she persisted, till love and hope together created
their own reward. And before your experiment was
abandoned, did you take sufficient pains to warrant its

success? It is not enough to gather an expectant group,
and assume that you shall be able to address them. No
multitude of guests will conjure a banquet from an empty
board; nor will the largest congregation elicit an interesting discourse from an unfurnished mind. But many
imagine that a pocket Bible is a magician's mirror, and
needs only to be opened in order to summon up forgotten
facts, appropriate similitudes, and powerful arguments;
and they are mortified if they do not find in every text
a talisman. None could depend on Divine assistance
more devoutly, nor court the influences of the Comforter
with more ardent aspirations, than did the subject of
this memorial; but she sought them in her study as well
as in her school-room; and then, when her mind was
matured as to the meaning of the passage, and replenished
with materials for expounding and enforcing it, she was
able to look up for the promised help with calm and
undistracted confidence. So deeply interested was she
in this employment, and so persuaded that God would
bless it, that her leisure was delightfully occupied in
searching the Scriptures, and in preparatory meditations;
and till her health gave way she was never daunted by
the frequent sensation of fatigue. May we not hope that
her modest labors will afford some encouragement or
guidance to that growing number among the refined and
the leisurely who "have compassion on the multitude?"

She now paid frequent visits to her son-in-law and
daughter, in Suffolk. She delighted in the primitive nooks,
the bosky dells, the winding lanes, and little corn-clad
hills which make up one of the most picturesque and
sequestered of Old England's counties; and many a
musing walk she took, when the tide was full, along the
grass-girdled creek which stretches away from the grounds
of Stutton to the ancient seaport of Harwich. But beyond

the beautiful landscape, she found materials of much
interest in the homely villagers. At first, when she stepped
into their cottages, as she had been accustomed to do at
Luss, and in her district of St Luke's, in Edinburgh, they
could scarcely comprehend her errand. But when from
her conversation and the tracts which she gave them,
they found that her motive was pure benevolence, their
gratitude was as great as their surprise. She found
amongst them not a few members of the Wesleyan
Society, and they begged that she would return to their
houses in the evenings, and explain the Scriptures when
the work of the day was ended. With such requests she
gladly complied; but so many of the neighbors came
together, that she was obliged to place restrictions on
their zeal, and limit the attendants to a certain number.
The impressive way in which she read the Word of God,
and her enforcement of its truths so clear and earnest,
are still vividly remembered among them; and there is
reason to believe that some got real benefit. To these
engagements there are a few incidental allusions in her
Diary. Thus:—

"*Stutton House, June 21,* 1840. — I feel that I have
been sent here with a message to many. The people
gladly receive my books and tracts, and I have seen some
Christians among the Methodists.

"*July 12.* — On Thursday I met with a number of the
villagers in a cottage. I read the second chapter of
Ephesians, with explanation, and prayed with them. And
now we are to separate, perhaps never to meet in this
world: Oh! to meet on the right hand of the Judge!

"*Aug. 27.* — Yesterday was greatly interested in speaking to one of the villagers, who said that she had back-
slidden from God. May I have been sent to her with a
blessing!"

Among the Church of England clergymen with whom she became acquainted in Suffolk, she was much pleased with the active benevolence of the Rev. J. B. Wilkinson, of Holbrook, and the missionary zeal of the late Mr Nottidge, of Ipswich; and, with all her preference for the simple worship of the Scottish Church, nothing more delighted her than to find affectionate preaching and devotional fervor elsewhere.

"*Oct. 1.* — We went to church at Ipswich to-day, to hear Mr R——, a young minister, who is doing much good there. I was much pleased and cheered to hear the truth plainly, ably, and judiciously preached; and he read the service beautifully. My heart unites with all in every denomination in whom I see the Spirit's impress. This is truly a magnet to me. Spent some hours in my room agreeably afterwards, and read, as usual, to the servants."

From the same place she thus wrote to a very dear invalid friend:—

"1839. I have gone into a few of the cottages with my little messengers of peace — the tracts, and they give me a hearty welcome: but I scarcely know what to say to them, they seem to have so few ideas in common. It appears to me that they comprehend little, while they assent to everything. However, they take the tracts with thanks, and sometimes the cheering thought occurs that I have not come so far for nothing. Who knows what God may bless? . . . . . But, my dear young friend, as well in our winters as our summers the foundation standeth sure; 'Christ is all.' With Him is no variableness, neither shadow of turning. Precious truth! Let us rest upon it, and cease from the vain endeavor to find anything in us that can give the shadow of hope. Abiding hope must be fixed on an object that changeth not: we change daily, hourly: He remains glorious in holiness eternally. And this Perfection is in the Court of Heaven our representative. Can we want more? Shall we say, I will add a few of my virtues and graces to the account? When we are guilty of this folly, we weary ourselves seeking for them, for they cannot be found, and our harp hangs upon the willows. But we resume the songs of Zion when we look *entirely* from ourselves to 'the Lord our Righteousness.' How is it with you, dear A.? Can you rejoice in the Lord always? If not, experience will teach you that living on frames and feelings will not do; that comfort ebbs and flows with these; and that you equally delude yourself when you take comfort from the feeling of nearness to God, or when you lose it because you lack that joy in devotional exercises, which is nevertheless extremely desirable and much to be prized. This, however, is distinct from joy in Christ crucified, and in Christ our Righteousness; and it is very possible to feel little heart for prayer and to mourn an absent God, and yet to stand firm on the sure Foundation, rejoicing in Christ, and never doubting that we are complete in Him."

"*Stutton House, June 10,* 1840. — My dearest A., I received your letter with mixed feelings of pleasure and pain. I was glad to hear from yourself, and thankful to find that the Lord is still at your right hand; but I was disappointed at the account you give of your health. Dearest A., I do fear your wish will be granted, and that God intends to take you shortly to himself. But when God wills it so, and you are willing, shall I say Nay? I trust not. 'His infinite wisdom can never mistake.' *As thou wilt*, I desire to say, both regarding myself and all who are dear to me. Difficult the duty is, but God can impart the ability to perform it. I rejoice in the

grace given to you, dear young friend; and I must repeat,
Oh, to be a partaker of it! I know God will never leave,
never forsake you. Through life, through death, throughout eternity, that same God will be your All who now
cheers you in the trying hours of sickness.

"Much, very much mercy follows me. I only lack
greater nearness to God, a sense of His presence and
love, and greater joy in Him as my chief Good and only
Portion. If He is pleased to deny me these inestimable
privileges, I have no right to expect them: and even then
I cleave to the covenant, and to Him who 'of God is
made to me Righteousness.' You see I have not forgotten Mr Smeaton's text. It often comes to my remembrance with power, still. No other righteousness have I;
no better can I want, nor do I desire."

"*June 30.* — I am still at Stutton, but expect soon to
move to London — not exactly the place I should have
chosen; but all is well. God, my God, can be with me
there, or anywhere, as He has been here. He has been
present lately without any outward means save books,
and I have enjoyed many a stroll by the river side with
my Bible, more than I have often enjoyed in the house
of God with the greatest spiritual advantages. I feel,
too, that I am sent to others, and think I see some fruit;
and *when, where, how* Thou wilt, is what I desire to say,
regarding any change of residence."

The years 1839 and 1840 are years much to be remembered in Scotland's spiritual history. God was not then
"a stranger in the land;" and at Kilsyth, in Dundee and
Perth, in Roxburghshire, and in Breadalbane, such immediate and unwonted effects accompanied the preaching
of the Gospel, that nothing seemed impossible to faith
and prayer. Nor were they only ministers who preached
with assurance of success; elders of the Church and

private Christians were roused to fresh exertions on behalf of their neighbors. In conjunction with some others, Lady Colquhoun spent a considerable portion of her time in visiting a neglected district of the New Town of Edinburgh; and from the transparent sanctity of her character, and the commanding sweetness of her manners, few visitors were more welcome or more impressive. The resumption of these labors is thus recorded in her Diary:—

"*4 Moray-place, Nov. 24.* — I have on hand much new duty, having undertaken to visit, as before, the poor in Thistle-street, and also to visit weekly, in turn with some others, the school there. And I have joined a prayer-meeting of ladies, who meet every Thursday. Lord, grant Thy blessing and assistance! Without Thee I can do nothing. Strengthen for Thine own work a poor helpless creature. Last week I was much encouraged by hearing that one I had visited, and whom I found in a very careless state, had died hopefully."

In letters to her like-minded correspondent, she occasionally notices the more interesting cases; and although it would be premature to publish what she says regarding hopeful individuals till they have given that most decisive evidence, "perseverance to the end," the reader may obtain a glimpse of the home missionary in the following extracts:—

"I have seen ———. It seems the old Highland woman next door is her sister, and by her account (for she has so little English that I cannot judge of her), the sister is in the same state of anxiety in which she herself was formerly, praying night and day for her soul's salvation. ——— told her. 'Perhaps ye'll get peace in a moment.' The old woman has a son and daughter-in-law who have come from Glasgow to stay with her. They were

notorious drunkards, but are keeping sober. ——'s great
anxiety was that I should speak to them all. 'Oh, will
you speak to them? they think I'm *by mysel'*.'* So, to
secure the young man's being in, I went at their dinner-
hour, but said to ——, 'I fear I shall interrupt their
dinner.' 'Oh!' said she, 'if they were to want their dinner
for a twelvemonth, what does that matter?' I thought
they all seemed affected, especially in prayer, when I
earnestly pled for sinners, and the young pair promised
to go and hear Mr M. I gave the old woman some Gaelic
tracts, and she began to read them instantly. —— told
me of a very interesting case opposite: a poor woman
with five children, whose husband is a perfect reprobate.
She is interested for her soul, but he will not let her
attend on ordinances; and the last communion he scolded
her so, because she was dressed to go, that she was quite
unfitted for the Lord's table, and stayed at home."

"*Friday.* — I made out a visit to the poor persecuted
woman I wrote you of, and she was telling me some of
her grievances, when in came her husband, a forbidding-
looking hackney-coachman. He started back and went
to another room. I sent for him, saying, if he liked to hear
it, I was going to read the Bible. He came in, and I
chatted a little first, and he related a long story how ill
he had been used by a man whom he had once befriended.
I took the opportunity and said, 'You may often meet
with ingratitude from man, because we are sinful
creatures; but go to God and trust Him, and He will
never forsake you'; and then I read my little portion as
usual with prayer; and certainly my hardened acquaintance looked softened, for I saw him wipe his eyes."

Writing to the same friend, August 27, 1838, she says:—
"The few words, 'God is love', have been delightfully

* Beside myself.

on my mind lately. I cannot give you the impression that
has been given me; for I feel that it is by the Holy Ghost
(the reality of whose influences I am more and more convinced of), and that in speaking to others or they to us,
of what this blessed Agent teaches, we have no power
to bring to the mind of another what we ourselves
experience. I should like much to know Mr M'Cheyne.
Your account of his pretty idea regarding the wilderness
is so like him, I think I could have told who said it."

The diary of August 19 alludes to the same text :—
"For some days 'God is love' has been delightfully
impressed upon my mind, and I have been enabled very
much to give up the creature. I saw the greatness of
God's love *to me*, and from His being love — the essence
of it — I conceived how He could love multitudes, even
as we do one or two. We have not love enough to give
to many, but God's love is to all His children equally
strong to that which we have to a very few, and probably
much greater. How sweet!"

Under the same date she apprises her friend of a new
volume which she was preparing, "The World's Religion
as contrasted with genuine Christianity". It appeared in
the following winter, and in 1835 had been preceded by
"The Kingdom of God". "The World's Religion" was
Lady Colquhoun's last publication, and though in its
structure and contents wholly distinct, its title will remind
the reader of that book which she had reason to prize
beyond all human authorship, the "Practical Christianity".
This fondness for a first love is an interesting feature of
advancing years; and though the shadows are reversed, it
is pleasant to know that "the light of evening-tide" is often
richer and warmer, yes, and more radiant with hope, than
the morning spread upon the mountains. In broken

health and in life's decline she penned this wisest and happiest of all her works, to teach her *youthful* friends where to look for happiness. She there mentions an incident which her father once told her. It was the time when Lord Melville was so high in office as to be the envy, or the idol, of his Scottish countrymen. He had asked Sir John Sinclair to spend New Year's Day with him at Wimbledon, and having slept in the house the previous night, Sir John repaired in the morning to the chamber of his host, to wish him a happy new year. "It had need be happier than the last," was the stateman's answer, "for I cannot recollect a single happy day in it." And though the pious authoress does not obtrude her own experience, it is right that it should now be known. Under the date February 3, 1839, we find her recording in her diary:—

"This day three years ago, my dear husband departed from me. These years have been years of mercy. No misfortune has befallen me; I have wanted for nothing, and grace, I trust, has grown." And all throughout there predominates a cheerful and confiding love, as of one in whose future there could be no real evil, and who had found a Friend possessed of all-sufficiency.

The following year commences:—

"*Edinburgh, Jan. 5*, 1840. — A precious Sabbath, with something of the Spirit's influence in public and private. Mr Moody preached twice from 'Redeeming the time because the days are evil.' He began with a striking observation, that time has risen in price, as every commodity does when it grows scarcer. He had heard of a heathen monarch to whom a sorceress brought nine volumes of a book, demanding a high price for them. Thinking it too much he refused, and she burned three, demanding for the six the price of the nine. He still declined to give it, and she burned three more, asking the full sum for the remaining three. He began to think there must be something extraordinary in the books, and fearing to lose them all, he gave for the three the price he had refused for nine. So time, as it dwindles, grows more valuable."

And now we gladly avail ourselves of a few extracts from letters to her endeared correspondent, Miss S. :—

"*13 Cumberland-street, Hyde Park,*
"*London, Aug.,* 1840.

"Many thanks for your prayers. Perhaps you prayed for me last Sabbath. I was detained at home by my cold, and spent most of the day in my own room; yet God was very present, and my heart was with Him. It was impressed upon me, Some one prays for me — perhaps my dear A. One verse I met with in the course of reading was sweetly consolatory: I think it is Watts's :—

> " 'Jesus! I throw my arms around,
>   And hang upon thy breast;
> For I have sought no other home,
>   And found no other rest.'

This rest, dearest A., abides. You are about to move where you would not go (to Madeira), but your home —your rest, goes with you. Strive to cast away all anxiety, just as if you saw the Saviour's arms around you. I need not remind you, Be careful for nothing, but make known your requests. He would have you without carefulness. Trust Him — try Him; I know it will go well with you. I had a letter lately from my dear friend in Canada, Mrs Scott. She relates what is to me very interesting: that she had read an account of Kilsyth which I gave her to a man from Glasgow who was working there, but who, with his wife, had become much addicted to drinking. He was so much struck as to change his conduct ever since, and she has hopes of the conversion of both. I have just read in the newspapers that there has been a tremendous hurricane at Liverpool, and not over on Tuesday, when I meant to have been there. Thus, by this cold I have been spared the inconvenience of remaining there, or of sailing for Scotland, when neither safe nor pleasant. 'Trust in the Lord for ever.' "

TO THE SAME.
"*Rossdhu, Oct. 6,* 1840.

"Whether life or death be in your cup, I cannot tell. My impression certainly is, that He has thus early ripened you for glory with the view of taking you to Himself. And is it not a blessed thing that I can tell you this without the fear of agitating or distressing you? — that while to you 'to live is Christ, to die is gain?' But, it may be, years of usefulness await you; and I, who am old in years, and who, having long known the precious-ness of salvation by grace, ought to be also ready, may be taken first, and may welcome you as you 'enter in through the gates into the city.' I often think of this passage. Two gates seem evident: Christ the door, and the gate of death. There is no admission but through these gates, and, when these are passed, no impediment. Oh, the joy of the entrance when the gates *are* passed, and the poor doubtful believer finds himself safe in the city!"

TO THE SAME.
"*Rossdhu, Nov. 11,* 1840.

"You ask me for texts. The eleventh chapter of John,

with all the particulars, as explained in Henry's Commentary, has been much blessed to me lately — particularly what is said of our Lord's love. 'He whom thou lovest is sick.' No doubt upon the subject; Christ's love must have been evident to all. 'Now Jesus loved Martha, and her sister, and Lazarus.' It is simply told; yet carries the conviction that the Apostle saw this love. I have been apt to think too much of Jesus' love as pity and benevolence; its reality never struck me so much as lately in reading this passage. And if we had an Apostle to tell our story, he might say with equal truth, 'Now Jesus loved A. and her friend, and that other, and each of His redeemed ones on earth.' I know this truth has been brought home to my mind by the Holy Ghost; and, dear young friend, I cannot convey my meaning to you unless He is pleased to reveal it. Perhaps you knew it long ago."

TO THE SAME.

"*Rossdhu, Sept. 8,* 1841.

"The proposed union for prayer is interesting, and I shall try and not forget Madeira. I feel, also, some anxiety for our dear Scotch Church. We used to agree not to talk of it; but it now appears as if its downfall were approaching. The Moderate party push on the decision as to which side shall constitute the Establishment; and if they are to constitute our Church, woe to many a destitute district which can have access to no other preachers. Yet God reigns, and is 'Head of the body — the Church.' There will still be Christ's Church, and possibly there may be a great reviving among us. Amen.

"I heard lately from my dear friend in Canada, Mrs Scott, and she asks with much interest about you. She is a 'sister,' and you will meet in glory. How many will be there whom we shall love as much as those who are dearest to us now! Love is the fulfilling of the law, and there will be no scarcity of love in heaven — "beloved and loving all t' embrace.' Often do I think, could I perfectly love God I should be quite happy: but here again, I see no hope till taken to a better world. I can no more excite this love than I can fly. I can only say, Lord, let me love Thee; permit me to love Thee; enable me to love Thee. And if there be the faintest commencement of this love, it is Himself hath done it. 'You hath he quickened who were dead'; He will perfect what concerns us, and will not forsake the work of His own hands. This is my hope — my only hope, but it is a noble hope; '*God's* workmanship, *created* in Christ Jesus unto good works, which *God* hath before *ordained*, that we should walk in them.' "

TO THE SAME.
"*20 Charlotte-square, March 9,* 1842.

"Mr Burns' preaching has much power accompanying it; he is truly in earnest, and I hear his ministrations are blessed. Mr M'Cheyne administered the sacrament beautifully, and, oh, how he prayed for our dear pastor!* It must have reached many hearts. He also read to us one evening Mr Moody Stuart's second Pastoral Letter, and interspersed it with remarks of his own, very sweet and apposite. It seemed like the two friends speaking to us together. I never saw Mr M'Cheyne so solemn and spiritual. One great loss in Mr Burns is, that he takes no superintendence of the parish; he is always preaching elsewhere. But the elders are exerting themselves, and seem to feel their responsibility. — And now, how joyful to know that all these things are under God's control,

* Then in impaired health, and also residing at Madeira.

and not beneath his notice! A verse in Psalm civ. has
often been food for me. Here it is, dear A., you shall
partake of my bread:—

> " 'Of Him my meditation shall
> Sweet thoughts to me afford;
> And as for me, I will rejoice
> In God my only Lord.' "

It was in this year that a new system of Sabbath-
desecration was introduced in Scotland, and with deep
sorrow Lady Colquhoun in her dairy records:—

"*March 13.* — The day when the Sabbath trains begin
to run on the Edinburgh and Glasgow Railway."

On this point so strongly did she feel, that the next
time she has occasion to travel betwixt the two cities,
she hired post-horses, rather than employ a conveyance
which systematically violated the Divine command. She
was then in feeble health, and the journey consumed
two days instead of as many hours; but in carrying out
a strong conviction of duty, few thought so lightly of
personal convenience or comfort as Lady Colquhoun.

We shall close this chapter with a few additional extracts
from her Journal, as further illustrations of the state of
her mind during the period which it embraces:—

"*Edinburgh, Dec. 3*, 1837. — I had an affecting request
sent me this evening, to pray for Mrs Macdonald, of
Clanranald, who is thought dying. I did so repeatedly
and truly. This whole day has been more entirely spent
in religious exercises than I sometimes can manage. O
Lord, bless me with life. I desire spiritual, eternal life.
No outside work, but inward, enlightening, enlivening
grace. For this I thirst.

10th. — And in a measure this has been bestowed

to-day. I arose early, and prayed fully and earnestly, with something of God's presence. I feel the love of God strongly, and more especially for what He is — yes, Lord, I *do*, I cannot but love Thee. I see a glimpse of Thy beauty. I am constrained to say, 'Whom have I in heaven but Thee? and there is none upon earth I desire beside Thee.' I delight to repeat that I love Thee, for Thou only art holy. Oh, how captivating is perfect holiness! 'My soul doth magnify the Lord, and my spirit hath rejoiced in God my Saviour.' These feelings continued with me at times the whole day, and partly for some days after. Mrs Macdonald is wonderfully better.

"*17th.* — I have been tried the end of last week by something distressing, which was evidently removed by prayer to-day. I have the pleasure to hope I am useful to some young people here.

"*Feb. 18*, 1838. — The Spirit's influence was with me, particularly after dinner, and at prayer at night. How sweet it is to feel God's presence, and to pour out the heart before Him! How marvellous that He hears, and has many times heard, *me!* Oh, the praise of the glory of His grace! I do exceedingly rejoice in the thought that it shines brightly in what He has done for me. God shall be glorified in me, even eternally! So would I have it. Even so, Lord, for so it seems good in Thy sight.

"*25th.* — Tolerably spent, but I was enabled to pray with my whole heart at night. This is indeed cause of much joy to me. I rejoice in this communion with Jehovah. It *is* my joy. I prayed most earnestly for the Spirit's influence, and feel it shall be given me, for God hath said so. Oh, the preciousness of the promises!

"*March 18.* — To-day I feed upon the bread of life. God gave Mr Moody to give me. The afternoon sermon, upon Christ suffering the just for the unjust, was truly impressive. Oh, to think that He *suffered!* We forget the meaning of the word; and that it was the just, the ONLY just and holy One. For this blessed purpose, to bring us to God! Bring *me*, blessed Saviour, to God, even very near to God. I am afar off, make me nigh. And now I delight in approaching unto God.

> " 'When shall i near
> Unto thy countenance approach,
> And in God's sight appear?' "

"*May 20.* — To-night I prayed with the most intense desire for the influences of the Spirit. Oh, my God, such prayer must be heard! I know it. I believe it. Thou hast said it. Prayer like this is *from* the Spirit's influence. It is *given*. I could not pray for grace once. Thanks, O my God, for the desire, the earnest, longing desire. I *believe* that I receive the Spirit, and I shall have it. No presumption here, it is only crediting the promises.

"*Rossdhu, July 15.* — I hoped to be well enough to go out to-day, and would have been able had the day been favorable. But as it is, I could not venture to church, or to the school. I grieve on account of the school. Prayed in earnest, and was led delightfully to meditate on the freeness of redemption; gave up faith *as a work*; leant on the promise irrespective of *anything*, and prayed, receiving Christ as all, for justification, sanctification, and eternal life. Felt strengthened.

"*Sept. 23rd.* — Something of the Spirit's influence seemed apparent to-day. I prayed and spoke and read with comfort, and feel as if some of God's children were interceeding for me.

"*Edinburgh, Feb. 24th.* — Another day when the Spirit was given me. I was much interested last night in reading a little book, 'Successive Bereavements', being

an account of the death of four children who died in the
Lord, by their father, Mr Beith. The simplicity and the
strength of the faith of these lambs of Christ's flock
struck me forcibly, and I thought, Why may not I confide
just as simply, as strongly? My visits to the poor in
Thistle-street interest me. Some look anxious for instruction.

"*March 10th.* — Joy in God and confidence in Christ
has been in some degree my experience. A mission, which
is about to be undertaken by the Church of Scotland, to
inquire into the state of the Jews, interests me. I have
given £50 towards defraying its expense. Mr M'Cheyne
and Mr Bonar are going. Lord, bless and prosper this
undertaking, and gather in thine Israel.

"*Rossdhu, Sept. 22nd.* — This morning I found God
in prayer. Was at church and the school, where I read
an account of the recent revivals which have taken place,
not only in Scotland, but in many other places. Oh! for
a plenteous rain to refresh the weary heritage.

"*Edinburgh, Sutherland's Hotel, Nov. 2nd.* — I feel
gratified at the reception I have met with from many
Christian friends. I trust for a blessing on the approaching
communion, and that God has not brought me here to
be *quite alone* without some good end in view. I have
had great enjoyment in hearing Mr Wm. Burns twice —
that young man who has lately been made the instrument
of doing so much good by awakening hundreds at Kilsyth
and Dundee. I sought God in several ordinances this
week; but listening to Mr B., I did find Him. The Spirit
accompanies the word from his lips. Lord, I praise Thy
name for raising up such an instrument, so spiritual and
so young. I earnestly pray for a blessing to-morrow.
Lord, *many* cry unto Thee for the outpouring of Thy
Spirit : Lord, hear!

"*4, Moray-place, Nov. 24th.* — To-day I seemed to arise with God's blessing. He was present in prayer in the morning, which I could not but particularly notice, as I slept too long, and was hurried. I enjoyed also the morning service, when Mr Moody lectured from the 14th chapter of Proverbs. I have much new duty on hand, having undertaken to visit, as formerly, the poor in Thistle-street, and also to take charge with some others of the school there, by weekly visiting in turn. I have joined a prayer-meeting of ladies, who meet every Thursday. O Lord, grant Thy blessing and assistance. Without Thee I can do nothing : strengthen a poor helpless creature for Thine own work. I was much encouraged by hearing last week that one I had visited, and whom I found in a very dead state, had died hopefully.

"*Dec. 15th.* — I have witnessed to-day the impressive service of the baptism of a Jew. He was baptized by Mr Moody. His name is Philips. The sermon preparatory was very interesting, from Galatians iii. 7, 14.

"*29th.* — The peace of God is with me. An invitation from Christians in Glasgow to join with those here on the morning of the Sabbath in prayer for the outpouring of the Spirit everywhere has been useful to me. I feel as if it must be granted, and rejoice. I rest on Christ this evening, leaning on Him helpless, and out of Him hopeless.

"*Wednesday, Jan. 1*, 1840. — Upon a review of the past year, compared with the preceding one, I think there is less religious feeling in it, and yet I cannot complain of much deadness either. I have a sweet sense that God has been with me wherever I went, and I have seen His providence conspicuously.

"*Feb. 2nd.* — Prayed in truth, but I was not so much impressed as last Sabbath. The accounts of religious

revivals from many places are most encouraging. Every
week we hear of some new one, where those before dead
are earnestly seeking after God. Glasgow, Perth, Dundee,
Cupar, St. Andrew's, Dunfermline, Ancrum, Kilsyth,
Fintry, Kelso, Lewis, are among the number. Bless the
Lord, O my soul!

"*April 19th.* — Since writing here I have been laid up
with influenza, and have been four Sabbaths out of
church. I have great cause for thankfulness that everything has been amply bestowed upon me which I could
want in this illness, and that my mind has not been dark.
I have felt the presence of God, have been enabled to
pray to Him, and I have seen the preciousness of the
Saviour, and been enabled to cast myself on Him, for
time and for eternity. My Sabbaths have been happily
spent. To-day I am out of bed, though weak, and I am
resting on the Rock of my salvation fully and joyfully.
An account of the last hours of Mr Simeon, that eminent
servant of God, has been blessed to me, and I have been
brought nigh to God in prayer. This is the Sacrament
week. I anxiously wish to be enabled to attend during the
services.

"*April 23rd.* — I have been able to go once to church
to-day, and was greatly blessed through Mr M'Cheyne's
ministrations.

"*Rossdhu, Sept. 6.* — I have felt the presence of God
since coming here, and still feel it. I met the grown-up
people at our school to-day, and read to them as formerly,
but with less interruption to my own devotional feelings
than often before. There was a good attendance. Oh,
that God would bless my poor attempts to do them good!
This week I expect much company. God can prevent my
losing by it in spiritual things.

"*Oct. 11.* — A clergyman from America preached at

Luss to-day, and very well, from 'He *must* increase'. Joyful news! Oh, for the increase of the latter days! I have earnestly prayed and longed, since returning here, for a spiritual blessing on this parish and neighbourhood, and do hope to be heard in God's good time.

"*Nov. 1.* — Another Sabbath detained at home by the weather, and being afraid of bringing back my cold, I am spending my sacred hours as I can, and have lately found much nearness to God, accompanied by realizing conceptions of the love of Christ, which seemed to arise from the frequent mention in the Evangelists of Christ's love to His disciples, who were with Him on earth, particularly Mary, Martha, and Lazarus. We think often of Christ's love more as if it were pity and benevolence, than the real feeling of Love.

"*Jan. 3*, 1841. — Another year is gone. Last year and the one preceding it have been wonderful, from the increase in our Church of vital godliness. In many places the Word has been remarkably blessed to the conversion of sinners. It is generally thought that a time of distress approaches. Oh! to have 'my loins girt about, and my lamp burning.' I am again at home, but though debarred from God's house, have received more of the Spirit's influence. I feel a great emptiness of self, and I delight to feel it. I would hide myself altogether in the unspotted robe that Christ hath bought for me and all His.

"*20 Charlotte-square, Thursday, Feb. 4*, 1842. — The fast-day at St. Luke's. I have been striving truly to humble myself. I feel grieved that my sins and shortcomings are so many, and that I am so little what I would be. Looking at myself as an aged disciple of Christ, and for so many years His, what can I cry but 'Lord, forgive?' I feel this day very low in God's sight, but 'leaning on the Beloved'.

"*Rossdhu, July 10.* — I found my God in reading, meditation, and prayer. My prayers have been lately more devotional, and to-day I pled as on last Sabbath, and frequently during the week most earnestly for the Spirit on myself, my family, this neighbourhood, Edinburgh, Mr Burns in connexion with this, the Jews, the continent, the world, &c. Oh! Lord, hear, hearken, and do. Amen.

"*Aug. 7.* — No service at Luss, being Arrochar Sacrament. At first my frame was dull and stupid, but I was revived in reading the Word and prayer; and Traill's Sermons were again blessed to me. Two observations of his struck me, that death is the way to *life*, as by the death of Christ we live, and it is by our own death we enter life. Another was, that Christ in the soul *is* eternal life — 'This is the true God, and eternal life'.

"*132 George-street, March 12*, 1843. — This morning I had strong desires that the services of this day, in St. Luke's particularly, should be blessed to many, and could scarcely give up praying for this; and once was led to conclude that it would be so, for prayer, when real, is an index of the mind of God. These thoughts have come to me — That as God will glorify His Son, so if we are His children, glory naturally follows; that there is an identity of feeling in the Church below and above, respecting the conversion of sinners, joy in heaven and on earth over one that repenteth. And likewise much in 'Howe's Blessedness', upon the joy of *feeling* the soul in health, and the disease of sin completely cured in a future state, has been refreshing to me.

"*March 26.* — To-day I have been fed in the Sanctuary, and in private God has been near. Christ very precious. I read with delight this evening 'Dyer on following the Lamb'. I feel my relation to Him; I exult in it. I prayed at night with my whole soul, and just as a man would converse with his friend. Blessed privilege! I heard this morning of the death of Mr M'Cheyne, of Dundee, which I deeply lament for the Church's sake. Lord, raise up many such laborers, and O bless spiritually the afflicted Church of Scotland.

"*April 29.* — The eve of a Communion Sabbath. I have just prayed in truth, and have hopes of 'joyful communion'. It will probably be the *last* in connexion with the old Establishment. Oh! for a blessing on ministers and people!"

CHAPTER VI

Favour is deceitful, and beauty is vain; but a woman that feareth the Lord, she shall be praised. — Proverbs xxxi. 30.

Christ leads me through no darker rooms
  Than He went through before :
He that into God's kingdom comes
  Must enter by this door.

Come, Lord, when grace hath made me meet
  Thy blessed face to see;
For if thy work on earth be sweet,
  What will thy glory be !

My knowledge of that life is small,
  The eye of faith is dim;
But 'tis enough that Christ knows all;
  And I shall be with Him.

                              Richard Baxter.

THE year 1843 saw the Church of Scotland split in sunder. From no dislike to State-connexion, but in avoidance of secular control, two-fifths of the clergy and half the population withdrew from the old Establishment. Hot controversy and strong excitement preceded this event, as every one would expect, who knows the national temperament, and who, when her religion is concerned, remembers how polemical the history of Scotland has ever been. But just as a glowing summer will occasionally elicit some lovely plant, of which the soil has long contained the dormant germ, or as a volcanic outburst

will condense into crystalline beauty the elements which
have been hitherto crudely diffused through the strata —
so, those who are careful to collect the finest specimens
of human excellence must look for them in periods when
the public mind has been stimulated, or when the apathy
of ages has been startled by some powerful revolution.
Apart altogether from the rightness of their cause, it will
be conceded that more munificence, self-sacrifice, and
missionary enthusiasm were developed by the day of the
Disruption than by a century of tame church-going and
tranquil sermonizing; nor, until they learned it in the
furnace of affliction, did ministers and people know how
dear they were to one another, nor how intense was that
relation which bound them to their common Lord and
Lawgiver.

It so happened that in their capacity as members of
the Indian Female Education Society, Lady Colquhoun
and her friends were constrained to a miniature rehearsal
of the Disruption, some time before the greater event
transpired; and this first step, like the final one, she took
with her accustomed conscientiousness, irrespective of
fashion, and — which alone was painful — in some
instances, irrespective of personal friendship. But her
calm and independent mind had fully considered the
question; and, dear as the Scotch Establishment had ever
been to her, it was only dear so long as in sacred things
it owned itself amenable to none except its heavenly Head.
In following the cause of spiritual freedom, she believed
that she was only following the Guiding Pillar; and
though well aware that the ministers and elders whom
she chiefly esteemed would follow it also, it was a joyful
surprise to find such a multitude of the people prepared
for the movement. By giving impulse and outlet to the
piety of her remaining years, the Disruption is entitled

to form a date in her biography, as well as in many a private history.*

The first notice of this memorable day occurs in her journal :—

"*Rossdhu, May 28*, 1843. — I have been here upwards of a week; but neither this Sabbath nor the last have I enjoyed public ordinances. As was expected, the Disruption of our Church took place [May 18], when between four and five hundred of our devoted pastors gave up all for Christ, and rather than belong to an Erastian Church, left their homes and benefices. May a blessing, a great blessing, rest on themselves and their labors in 'the Free Presbyterian Church of Scotland', to which with them I now belong! Nothing is yet organized as to a stated ministry, and I did not think it right to attend in the old Establishment. Both last Sunday and to-day I have been enabled to read to my servants, and, though feeling the deprivation, have spent the day tolerably.

"*June 11*. — Mr Somerville came to Luss, and delightfully and very freely preached Christ, on Monday, at Arnburn, and on Tuesday in the village, in the open air, close to the church. Both times there was a good attendance, and many of the people seemed affected and struck. I myself felt much strengthened and invigorated."

For many years Lady Colquhoun had been praying for the parish of Luss, and her Journals show how confident she was that God would arise and have mercy upon that

* The history of the whole event has lately been published by Dr Robert Buchanan, in his interesting narrative, "The Ten Years' Conflict". The case has also been stated with singular perspicuity and force by members of other Churches; e.g., by the Hon. and Rev. W. B. Noel; by Mr Sydow, the King of Prussia's Chaplain; and by Dr Merle D'Aubigné, in his "Germany, England, and Scotland".

neighbourhood. In her own modest but useful labors, her prayer was partly answered; and in the plantation of the Free Church, she was spared to see it answered yet more fully. A congregation was organized; the Rev. Neil Stewart was ordained its minister; and on sites granted by her son, there now "stand most beautiful" the manse of the minister and the Church of the people. To some of these occurrences she thus alludes :—

"*Stutton, Sept. 10*, 1843. — Have lately found prayer answered in several particulars, which might be termed trifling, yet which cost me anxiety. Read this morning what I wrote here on prayer for Luss and its neighbourhood, Oct. 11, 1840; and may I not hope that these prayers are now answering?

"*Rossdhu, Nov. 19.* — Had the great joy to hear Christ fully and freely preached by our new young minister at the Arnburn, where the Free Church congregation meet. How many times have I prayed for a living life-giving ministry at Luss! What a difference it makes to me living here!

"*June 30*, 1844. — Again at the Arnburn, and heard Mr Stewart with great pleasure. There seemed an impression among the people. Oh, that God may appear in His glory among us! For this I long and pray. It is expected that the new church at Bandry will be opened next Lord's-day. These are great privileges. Lord, give the blessing! What can men do, even Thine own dear children? They are altogether powerless.

"*July 14.* — Last Lord's-day our Free Church was opened. I was nearly the whole day there. The services were impressive, and a great many from neighbouring parishes attended. Lord, bless this place, now set apart for Thy worship! May many sons and daughters be born unto Thee there!"

One day, during the building of the Free Church, she went in to see how the work was proceeding, and observing that one of the pews had a private door, and was also much larger and more elevated than the rest, she asked for whom it was intended. The carpenter said, "For your Ladyship and family." She immediately directed that the private door should be built up, and the pew made like its neighbors; "for," as she remarked, "there ought to be no distinctions in the house of God."

However, it was not only in procuring ministers for the parishes along the shores of Loch Lomond that the Disruption taxed the energy of Lady Colquhoun. For many years she had been the patroness and an influential director of various benevolent Societies in Edinburgh. One was an Association, already mentioned, for promoting Female Education in India, in connexion with the Scottish Missions there. Commenced by the pious and talented Mrs Wilson, of Bombay, the system soon ramified into all the eastern Presidencies; and, as opening the simplest and surest access to the homes of the Hindoos, it promises to be a most powerful instrument in India's moral regeneration. Lady Colquhoun set on it great value, and besides keeping in her own hand the minutes of the Society, with eminent wisdom and kindness she conducted the correspondence with its several agents. We think the two following letters to Miss Laing, at Calcutta, will be read with interest :—

"Rossdhu, July 17th, 1844.

"My dear Miss Laing, — I have very many times intended replying to your last acceptable letter, received some time ago; but I have had much to think of and to occupy me, from domestic trial, and other sources. Without adding any more on the subject, therefore, but that I hope you will believe it is not from any want of

interest in the cause, I proceed to say that the ladies of
our Society and myself were deeply affected with the
account of the distressing scenes through which you have
been called to pass in your separation from the Established Church. We, however, praise the Lord for the
support and direction afforded to you in this time of
need; and, now it is past, we think it may be the means
of enabling you to trust more stedfastly and implicitly
in time to come on that Almighty arm which is full of
power, and on that God whose name is 'Love'. We
immediately set to work to finish the articles you mention
as those which you are most in want of, and I hope before
this comes to hand, one box with many useful articles will
have reached you. Its value, I heard, was about £40.

"I am happy to find you are gathering again a few
orphans around you, and that your school increases.
It is precious work to teach a heathen child *anything*;
but, oh! my dear Miss Laing, could you implant the
knowledge of God, that is work of which an angel could
be proud. You may justly say you cannot. It is most
true. — But you can pray, and labor, and wait, and we
have ground to hope it shall not be altogether in vain.
May God multiply the fruit of your seed sown abundantly. Wait on the Lord, be of good courage, and He
shall strengthen your heart. It also gave us pleasure to
learn that you had received the present of a horse. All
these things are encouraging tokens for good. Our new
Society promises to do well. — Many of the auxiliaries
have joined us. Dr Wilson is a great assistance to us.
Pray remember me to Dr and Mrs Duff when you see
them. And with every Christian wish that the presence
and blessing of God may be with you,

"I remain, your sincere friend,
"JANET COLQUHOUN.

"I answered your former letter — I hope you received mine. We were glad to hear of the formation of your clothing society."

"*Rossdhu, Jan. 15th*, 1846.

"My dear Miss Laing, — I had the pleasure to receive your letter of a short time ago, and it is gratifying to hear that the Lord is in any way blessing your efforts in the barren soil of India. Before much good is effected, unless by a miracle of divine working, there must be time, and patience, and perseverance, here a little, and there a little. Yet it is very encouraging that there are hopeful symptoms among your little group, that they are, many of them, teachable and docile. And I often think that those whom you lost at the disruption may do great things yet, and that, perhaps, what you then suffered may turn out for the furtherance of the Gospel, as it turned your work into a new field, when possibly the seed *was* sown in the others. It is delightful to know that God worketh for His own glory whatever comes to pass. What times are these in which we live! Strange indeed to one like myself who can remember such a different state of things. There was in my young days a death-like apathy towards religion in most of those I was acquainted with. A few bright examples both in clergy and laity shone as lights in the darkness, but they were generally despised, considered fanatics, and, I think, often wanted sufficient *boldness* in their Master's work. They however, I mean the clergy, labored very assiduously, saw little fruit and *expected little*. A single conversion was thought a great thing and much spoken of. Now the fields everywhere seem ripe for the harvest. There is a shaking among the dry bones. How interesting is the intelligence from Switzerland, from France, from Germany, from Madeira, and many other districts and distant places. Surely God works, and who shall let it? I write thus to you, my dear young friend, because I would wish to encourage the hope that there is a blessing in store for India. The windows of heaven seem opening; put in your claim for a share of the refreshing shower. Oh! so I do, you say, but little has fallen yet. Well, hope on, wait on, aye, and work on. To use a homely simile, we make hay when the sun shines; so now appears to me the time when the Sun of Righteousness is about to arise with healing under His wings. It is a laborious life you lead, with the entire charge of so many young immortals; but after toil rest is sweet, and the rest that remains for the people of God will be most welcome to those who have borne the burden and heat of the day.

"It seems to me singular that a word of mine in my last letter should travel so far as India, and come wrapped up in that piece of paper with power to your mind, as you tell me 'Lean firmly on your Rock' did. But it shows who sent it. Oh! if we could act up to our professed belief, what different sort of Christians we should be! Happy, fearless beings, relying, resting, leaning on Him whose arm is power. But no; we think He may fail us in time of need, and so, like Peter, we begin to sink, till Jesus stretches forth His hand, and says, 'O thou of little faith, wherefore dost thou doubt?' I am not yet in Edinburgh, and so know less of the Society's operations; but, God willing, I expect to be there in about a fortnight. You had better, however, always address to this place, as it is sure of finding me. The concert for prayer is just over. I did not forget you, and indeed all missionaries, both in private and in the family. It lasted from Sabbath to Sabbath, and was well observed by the Free Church in daily meetings. Oh! for the

blessing! that outpouring of the Spirit for which we wait.
How is your little Jewess? does she learn quickly? Her
people are in an interesting state. I hope the set time to
favor Zion approaches. Remember me to Dr Duff when
you see him. I had the pleasure of knowing him in Scotland. And with every good wish that the Great Head of
the Church may own your efforts more and more,

"I remain, your sincere friend,

" JANET COLQUHOUN."

Then there was the Ladies' Society in Aid of the
Home Mission of the Presbyterian Church in Ireland.
In His providence God had opened to that Church a
peculiar opportunity of preaching the Gospel to the Irish-
speaking inhabitants of the west and south, and at a
time when few felt any interest in the subject, Lady
Colquhoun recognised in the tidings which she heard
an opening towards boundless usefulness. She succeeded
in comunicating to half-a-dozen friends something of
her own ardor, and founded an Institution which successive years have only rendered more imperiously
urgent. To her fellow-laborers in this cause she set a
noble example, by educating one of the converts, at her
own expense, for the Christian ministry; and by personal
communication with members of the Ulster Assembly,
she kept alive the zeal of herself and her colleagues. But
to her patriotic and practical spirit, still dearer, perhaps,
was the Gaelic School Society. Like her venerable father,
whose last thoughts were for the moral and religious
welfare of the Highlands, she had a warm attachment
to that people; and, knowing how many regions had been
spiritually enlightened, and how many thousands had been
scripturally instructed by this Society's godly teachers,
she gave it her most cordial and liberal support. But

each of these Societies was more or less shaken in that explosion which rent in twain the Established Church; and, though many statistics were long debated, two points were soon conceded : it was plain that the Free Church had all the missionaries, and equally plain that the Established Church had most of the moneyed men. And then it was that on the adherents of the new and scripless Institution was poured out that spirit of joyful contribution which, besides covering Scotland with a new system of school and sanctuaries, augmented its mission-staff, and invented schemes of pious enterprise as costly as they were original. Amongst the foremost in the ranks of liberal givers and instant doers, was Lady Colquhoun. Fully persuaded in her own mind, and alive to the peerless exigency, she commenced that series of sumptuous offerings so helpful to the cause, and so inspiring to its friends. Apart from local objects which mainly devolved upon her, if a Highland minister wrote for help to his people who had carted the stones and the timber, but who could not build the church; if a Lowland minister represented the case of some clever and pious youth who would fain go to college, but who could not pay the fees; if — as, alas! such tales were too frequent and too true — she heard of sufferings for conscience' sake, her wonderful purse was always open, and she so contrived to give that her gifts never hinted the self-denial of the sender. To herself money had now become a talent, and its right bestowment a means of grace; and, radiant with the bountiful spirit of this new dispensation, there was contagion in her cheerful offerings, as well as comfort in her calm and sagacious counsels. Inevitably she became the centre of those Societies of which she had been formerly the supporter; and, on the other hand, she rejoiced to find that her favorite schemes for India and Ireland had not suffered from the unwonted claims of Scotland.

Perhaps a manly gratitude is as rare as a princely munificence; but to the affectionate memory of one too high-minded to forget a favor, and too devout to regard Lady Colquhoun as his only benefactor, her biographer is indebted for an instance of her seasonable and discriminating kindness. It was in the summer of the Disruption, and when looking out for a Free Church minister for Luss, that the name of a young licentiate was mentioned to her. Though apprised that through excessive indulgence in study — for he had been reading eighteen hours a day — his health was broken, she sent for him. With some reluctance he came; but instead of the sturdy athlete which a country minister had need to be, there stood before her a spectral invalid. Two eminent physicians had told him that in less than nine months he must be in his grave, and the faithful warning had made him eager to work while it was day. From some cause or other, however, Lady Colquhoun was prepossessed with a sanguine hope that if rightly treated he would recover. She thought and prayed over his case, and sending for him again, propounded a scheme which she had devised for his benefit. She stipulated that he would put himself entirely in her hands, be guided by her advice, and use all means for convalescence at her cost. Of course, all preaching was strictly prohibited; the shattered student was ordered off to drink a famous mineral water; and after a year of rest and rustication he was ready to accept a cordial call to go and minister in a Highland congregation, amongst whom he has labored ever since, a vigorous and successful pastor. Having been favored with a perusal of the letters which Lady Colquhoun addressed to her young friend, if the following extracts strike the reader as the entire correspondence struck us, they will convey some idea of that delicacy and good sense, that piety and kindness which were so beautifully combined in her character.

"Sutherland's Hotel, July 1, 1843.

"Dear Mr ———, — On thinking over what I said to you yesterday, I fear I was not sufficiently explicit. I wish you to promise that after the two Sabbaths for which you are engaged, you will preach no more for some months, and save yourself in every way as much as possible. Nothing short of this will be of any avail, and it would be folly to deny yourself the satisfaction of doing much in the long-run, by perhaps one sermon. Therefore be firm in this respect, and be silent for the present. Depend upon it, to put steadily in force this resolution, requires more grace and strength from above than to follow your own inclination and preach the Word.

"Do not be very long in writing to me, as I shall be anxious to hear how the Almighty prospers our scheme, and trusting it may be His pleasure to grant you a long life of usefulness and many souls for your hire,

"I remain, your sincere friend," &c.

"Stutton House, Ipswich, Sept. 6, 1843.

"I received your letter this morning with real thankfulness; for I much feared my last had not reached you. I inclose ———, which I can assure you I give without any difficulty or deprivation to myself, and I am sure I may say with heartfelt pleasure. Could I be instrumental in perfecting your recovery, so that you may live to the glory of God and bring souls to the Saviour, how rich would be the blessing on this poor mammon of unrighteousness! For this I pray, and not without the hope that my prayer is heard. You shall not sell your books if I can keep them for you. God has brought your case under my notice most providentially. I praise His name for it. It is only an answer to many prayers that He would point out what He would have me to do.

"I am beginning to look to loved Scotland now, and think I shall not remain many weeks longer in England. I am living with a daughter and her family, in a pretty county, and where the air is delightfully clear and salubrious. But all will not make up for the want of those precious means of grace with which our favored land is blessed. May our afflicted Church have a double portion of the dew of Hermon descend upon her in her present afflicted and yet exalted state! She goes on prosperously, and 'with Christ in the vessel, may smile at the storm'."

"Stutton House, Sept. 25, 1843.

"Your last letter, gloomy although it is in some respects, gave me the sincerest pleasure, as it tells me you were beginning to derive benefit from the waters. May the Almighty continue to you their healing virtue, sending you health and cure! One thing I would with much earnestness *entreat*, that you will not think of leaving the place till medical men say there is no use in your remaining. I have a great fear of your but half-doing matters, and then all will be thrown away. One timely and persevering effort saves much. I know there will be somewhat more expense in your present residence; but to what better purpose can money be expended than in promoting the glory of God in the salvation of men? And do you not see that with your recovery this, by His blessing, may be intimately connected? My stock is not exhausted. God has given me means which many others do not possess; and in your case He has plainly said to me,

'Do this.' The debt is not to you; along with all I am and all I have, it is claimed by Him who loved me and gave Himself for me. Take, therefore, without scruple, what our Lord appoints as yours, and give him the praise.

"And now, as to the state of your mind. I read what you say with much sympathy. Oh! that God would enable me to send you a word from Himself! And first, I think it highly probable that the disordered state of the body has more or less connexion with it; and of this you will judge as the body recovers strength and tone. But from what you have written, as well as from what you said when we met, I should think there is something like impatience at the total inactivity — what you term uselessness, to which you are reduced. The desire of usefulness is good in itself; but, dear Mr ———, remember it is not for us to allot the times and the seasons when God shall employ our services. There is often a waiting time as well as a working time, and, if I mistake not, you will work 'double tides' shortly. Your present duty is to bear His will in silence, saying, When—where—how Thou wilt. But 'the face of God seems hid, and the Saviour less present and less precious'. Ah! this is indeed a bitter cup, and God alone can remove it. I have often thought that ministers must taste such things; or how should they know how to pity and console? This may be part of your education for the ministry; but such desertion shall not always last (Isai. liv. 7, 8, 10) and perhaps it shall be succeeded by bright and cloudless sunshine. In the meantime I would say, place yourself in the everlasting arms, whether God smiles or hides His countenance. Let faith supply the lack of feeling. He will not, He cannot cast you from Himself.

"Continue, dear Mr ———, to pray for Luss. It has been very dead and barren since I have known it, and is just beginning to show symptoms of life. I hear that Mr Stewart is gaining beyond the most sanguine expectations, and that there is a party much interested in his success. I am very glad my son has given them the most convenient site for a church."

                    "25, Charlotte Square, Feb. 19, 1845.

"My dear Mr ———, — My last letters seems, by God's blessing, to have been sent in season. May He give me a word in this one! Ah! let us never forget, God gives the word, whoever publishes it. It was cheering to me to hear such pleasing accounts from ———. There is enough to encourage faith and prayer. Seldom, if ever, does the servant of the Lord spend his strength for nought. It is wonderful to hear of your returning health. It is surely true what you say, 'the Lord is the author of this, and what language can express the gratitude due?' Let us magnify His name together. How many tales of wonder have God's people to tell ! And I have mine, even since I last wrote to you. You say you daily pray for my health of body and soul. I heartily thank you; nor was the liberty you experienced delusive, although you little thought of the circumstances I was placed in. Between two and three months ago I fell down stairs from a great height. It was about thirteen steps, and many have lost their lives from a less cause, or at least been seriously injured. But, wonderful to relate! not a bone was broken; and although a deep cut was close to one eye, the eye itself was uninjured. I was much bruised, and had to put on many leeches, and was confined to bed for a week. But never did I enjoy so much comfort on a sick bed. I was so overcome with gratitude for so merciful a deliverance, that I could do nothing but praise God, and He seemed present as if

beside me constantly. Mr Stewart was frequently with
me, helping me to praise, and was a great comfort to me;
and still I look back to that season as one of peculiar
joy. I am now perfectly recovered, and came here with
my son and the rest of the family about a month since.
My daughter has returned in good health, and enjoyed
her tour much. My little charge has thriven uncommonly
well, I am thankful to say. W. is also with us, and
well. What can I say more? All seems *well, well;* and
truly gratitude becomes a poor sinful creature for these
things. Yet one thing in some instances is lacking, and
that the chief thing, the one thing needful. This I would
desire to seek more and more for myself and others. I
have told you of my best time; I dare not tell you of
my worst, when the things of time eclipse the glory to be
revealed. But it shall not be always thus. 'God in His
glory shall appear,' and 'we shall be like Him, for we
shall see Him as He is.' Let us then fight on, 'faint yet
pursuing.' *You* have glorious work, and are a fellow-
laborer with God. This might give any one courage. I
inclose ten pounds to help to furnish your manse, as I
think you must have little to spare. I hope Mrs ———
likes her situation in the North. And with my sincere
prayers that grace, mercy, and peace may be with you in
Christ Jesus the Lord,

    "I remain, your true friend in the faith,
            " JANET COLQUHOUN."

In the early summer of 1844 a new and affecting duty
devolved on Lady Colquhoun. Her son, Sir James, had
been scarcely a year united to a lady* whose youth and

* The younger Lady Colquhoun was a daughter of Sir Robert
Abercromby, of Forglen, Bart. She died at Edinburgh, on the
3rd of May, 1844.

amiable dispositions promised a long duration of happiness, and the rejoicings over the birth of a first-born had hardly been celebrated in his hereditary domains —

> It was an April day; and blithely all
> The youth of nature leaped beneath the sun,
> When tidings came,
> A son was born; and tidings came again,
> That she who gave it birth was sick to death.

The infant, thus bequeathed to her maternal tenderness, became an object of unceasing solicitude to his fond grandmother; and if anything could have linked her spirit to the earth once more, that child would have been the tie. God blessed her anxious tending, and her little grandson grew in strength and stature. On the rare occasions when she was obliged to send him from under her immediate eye, a minute correspondence was maintained betwixt his attendants and herself; and in thinking and planning for the welfare of her precious charge, and in watching the developments of thought and affection, she lived delightfully over again a bygone era of her history.

The most appropriate contribution which a Christian lady can make to the cause of the Gospel is, when she "shows piety at home". It is related of a Scottish lawyer who rose to a high judicial station in England, that with infinite pains he had exchanged his vernacular pronunciation for a somewhat finical English accent; but when he became old and infirm, they say that nature cropped out again, and that it was curious to observe the broad Shibboleths of boyhood taking a late but ample vengeance on the euphuistic orator. And where piety is like Lord Loughborough's English — a thing picked up or put on — it is liable to similar casualties. In life's least guarded or least brilliant moments, in languor, in sickness, in moments of vexation, carnality triumphs over profession; and the spleen, or the passion, or the worldly-mindedness which was all unsuspected by the admiring committee or the parlour côterie, is revealed without scruple to the domestic circle. But the piety of Lady Colquhoun was such a pervasion that the minutest action and the most familiar moment could only reveal the Christian. "She behaved herself wisely in a perfect way, she walked within her house with a perfect heart"; and her uniform and attractive goodness commended the Gospel to her servants, to her family, and to the stranger sojourning within her gates.

For many years she had been in the habit of instructing her female servants every Sabbath afternoon; and, with her systematic perseverance, she often assembled them when feeble health made the exertion distressing to herself. Thus, in her journal we find her lamenting the levity which exhibited itself on one of these occasions; "for, considering the pain it cost me to speak to them, I felt it rather hard." But it was the tendency of such exertions for their welfare to conciliate the affection of her household, especially as they were the exertions of a most kind and considerate mistress. One evening, in Edinburgh, she rang the bell for her maid, but was told that she had gone out and had not returned. It was late before she arrived, and when she made her appearance Lady Colquhoun asked where she had been. "Taking tea with my mother," was the reply. But perceiving her embarrassed manner, Lady C. said, "Now, I know you are not telling me the truth"; and the young woman confessed that she had gone to a theatrical exhibition, which was later of ending than she had expected. However, it was true that the party had met at her mother's and taken tea beforehand; and she had intended to ask leave, but had not

found opportunity. Lady C. expressed her sorrow at the
occurrence, the more especially as she had never before
discovered in this maid any deviation from the truth.
She told her how much she disapproved of theatres, which
had ruined so many; and reminded her how one fault
usually leads to another; "and, C.," she added, "I have
just been praying for you." Tears started into the young
woman's eyes; and she begged forgiveness of her mistress,
solemnly promising never to be guilty of the like fault
again, a promise which she faithfully fulfilled. But
although she objected to such places of resort, and would
not allow her servants to spend the Sabbath in walks and
visits, she was liberal in allowing them other opportunities
of amusement, and was especially delighted when they
selected such recreations as tended to improve their minds.
The servant just mentioned had been attending some
evening lectures on astronomy, and Lady C. took great
pleasure in hearing all that she could remember, and in
helping her to understand them. And all the inmates of
her dwelling were so well aware of her benevolent feelings
towards them, that it is not wonderful that they received
with increasing gratitude her endeavours to promote their
truest welfare. "There was not one in the household who
did not love and reverence her, and who would not have
done anything to serve her." And if her instructions have
not been followed by lasting results in every case, none
who were connected with her can ever forget how holy
and unblameable was her daily demeanor.

With a few final extracts from her diary, we shall
conclude the active portion of this history. They will
supply some omissions in the narrative, and they will show
how the Lord was preparing his servant for her everlasting
rest.

"*Edinburgh, June 18*, 1843. — I am enjoying the rich

privilege of Mr W. Burns' ministrations, amidst much to
distract my thoughts. On the 14th my son, Sir James,
was married to Miss Jane Abercromby, an event which
has given me real pleasure. This day I have felt a little,
alas! *but a little*, of the Spirit's influence. I thought with
joyfulness of the will of God being *done in heaven*, and
that *there I* shall perfectly do it. Sensibly I feel my
inability to do anything right here — sin, sin mixes with
all I think, say and do. — Help, Lord!

"*Stutton House, July 16.* — To-day we attended Holbrook Church, and heard a good man, a German, preach.
I likewise read to the servants here both days. I have
great cause for thanksgiving that, on my journey here, I
was remarkably preserved from all danger and evil, and
that God is present. I found all well here, and my cup
runneth over.

"*Aug. 7.* — I have been striving to keep the Sabbath
holy, and have had some communion with God. We go
once to church, in the afternoon, as it is too far to go
twice to Holbrook, and I have Sabbath hours in the
morning, which I pleasantly spend in my own room.
To-day, especially, I was near to God, and met with Him
in Christ. How merciful, how joyful it is to think that
God is in every place, and is found of them that seek Him.
I read to the villagers again last week. I desire to do
something, whatever God will, and look up for a blessing.
My dear little James went to-day to church for the first
time. He is four years and three months. I am teaching
him the beatitudes in Matthew v. Have read to the
servants here as usual.

"*Sept. 3.* — I enjoyed my earlier hours much to-day,
reading the Bible and 'Howe's Blessedness' with prayer.
When *necessarily* absent from ordinances, how often have
I found God present! I was at Holbrook Church in the

afternoon, and was engaged with the servants, &c. in the evening. I have thought for some days of my security in Christ, that all is well *in time* and eternity. I felt upon a Rock.

"*20th*. — To-day my heart was cheered by hearing from several Christian friends — Lady Agnew, Mrs B., and Mr ———, particularly the last. I have felt so anxious that he may derive benefit from a plan I have suggested, and enabled him to put in practice, giving up all work for a time till his health is restored. He is a clergyman, lately licensed, but quite overborne by labor and studying, &c. eighteen hours a day. Thank God, he is better, and travelling about in Scotland. The news from Luss delight me : a Free Church is likely to be built, both there and at Arrochar; the people like Mr S———, and I trust he may prove a great blessing to the neighbour-hood.

"*Rossdhu, Tuesday, 28*. — Once more in my worthless way, have I partaken of the sacrament of the Lord's Supper, which was administered in the Free Church at Arnburn, last Sabbath. Mr Grant, of Roseneath, administered it,* and Dr Paterson, of Glasgow, preached yester-day. The services were all interesting. But, alas! my heart, although not dead, seemed deadened. I did however, greatly rejoice to see some signs of life in the people of this parish. O Lord! so be it.

"*127, George-street, Edinburgh, Monday, Dec. 25*. — Having omitted to bring my diary here with me, I have neglected writing for some weeks. Here I have been enjoying the highest privileges, for which at some periods of my life I would have given anything. I am in the same lodgings with Mr William Burns, having the two best floors, and he some rooms above. I am thus enabled to

---

* Before the ordination of the Rev. Neil Stewart.

attend his family worship night and morning, and he preaches regularly every Sabbath morning and twice during the week. To-day I was again feasted at his class for young women by his exposition of the question, What is God? I had before, nearly two years ago I think, heard part of this sublime subject with inexpressible delight, but left Edinburgh before he finished it, little hoping to hear any more. Now, if spared in health, I may hear the rest. Lord, grant it and the blessing!

"*31.* — Arrived at the end of another year, what can I say of myself in it? Perhaps I little know or think of my neglected duties, or many sins, but my heart does not smite me much; and yet I see others in labors much more abundant, and dear Mr Burns in this house, complaining bitterly of unprofitableness. It is probable that I am contented with a very low state both of feeling and labor. Let me press onward and forward. I took the family worship, as I do always on the Sabbaths, as Mr Burns is late of returning from the young men's class.

"*March 10*, 1844. — I find more than a month has elapsed, and I have omitted writing here. A passage from 'Dorney's Letters' came to me with power and comfort. 'The soul that is willing Christ should both save him and purge him, shall be saved and purged; and God cannot but account him clean from condemning guilt.' I have made an attempt to lead one, who I fear has been afar off, and have lent a book with faith and prayer ('Wilberforce's View'). From my being enabled to pray, I hope well in this.

"*March 17.* — My heart is rejoiced this evening by one of the servant-girls in these lodgings, whom I have been teaching, with the other, on the Sabbaths, telling me that what I said to her on prayer had been much blessed to her, and that she now found many opportunities to pray, and was happy in Christ. O Lord! truly I praise thee for this. Humbly and gratefully I thank Thee for making me the honored instrument in Thy glorious work. Bless and protect this poor girl, and build her up in the faith; and may she glorify Thee eternally!

"*April 14.* — An event of some importance to our family has occurred since I last wrote here — the birth of a son to my son, Sir James. His mother has been very delicate since; but all is in the hand of God; to Him I commit them, believing that He will do well. To-day I feel rather unwell, and am the less unwilling to remain at home, as (it is somewhat strange) I almost always find God more present during the Sabbath-day when thus confined, than when attending ordinances. Oh! it is *God*, not ordinances, I seek. Wherever He is present, I would be. And this day He *was* present, especially during the hours of the morning service. A letter received lately from Mr Denniston, of Jamaica, with some observations on walking with God, was blessed to me this morning.

"*28.* — A communion Sabbath. I was privileged to hear Mr A. Bonar, Mr Somerville, and Dr Duncan, on the previous days, but without any particular blessing; when, last night, a friend said she had been exhorted simply to receive Christ's broken body, as broken for *her* sins, and His shed blood as shed for *her*; and these few words brought joy and faith with them, which remained with me at the table; I was enabled to see a little of the Lord's beauty, and rejoice in Him. My daughter-in-law continues in a most precarious state; it seems uncertain whether or not she will recover. I have told her of the danger, and prayed with her several times.

"*May 5.* — A different Sabbath indeed from the last, Lady Colquhoun having departed this life on Friday afternoon. I witnessed her death, and have been since almost constantly with my son, at 132, George-street. The infant lives, and will be my precious charge. Thus a fresh line of duty and care devolves upon me, different, indeed, from what I should have sought. I am dumb; I open not my mouth : for God has done this. It is His way, therefore a right way.

"*May 19.* — I am beginning to awake from the dream of late events in my family, and am also beginning, I hope, to return to the Lord. I am certainly led in a way I would not in present circumstances; but it must be right. It goes to my heart when I recollect my dear little boy at Stutton, and my religious instructions of him last summer, and that now we cannot meet. One thing sweetly reconciles me — God did it. I was present at the opening of the Free Assembly, and enjoyed it much.

"*26.* — I was once or twice more at the Meetings of Assembly, which are truly solemn and interesting; but having caught cold, I am now debarred from them, and also from ordinances, to-day. I have, however, found God in private, both in reading and prayer. I lie very low because of shortcoming and sin; but I feel the value of the sacrifice offered for it, and see something of that righteousness which is unto all and upon all them that believe. Throughout the day my heart has rested on God as my portion. Oh, how precious! Thus at times creatures, the whole creation, keep their just place in my regard. I pant for more of this.

"*Rossdhu, August 11.* — Was much blessed in the house of prayer to-day, Mr Stewart preaching on the freedom of the Gospel offer, from John iii. 15. I had longed to hear him on this subject; and it was very joyful to me to hear Christ so freely and unconditionally preached at Luss. Lord, thou hast given us much in this Church, and in this thy devoted servant as our pastor;

yet all this may be without the blessing. For the Holy Ghost I pray; earnestly, unweariedly I pray for the descent of the Spirit upon this place and people. I pray in faith, and, looking up, expect the answer. I think I shall yet, if spared, write here that I am heard. O Lord, hasten the time!

"*Sept. 8.* — The three last Sabbaths Lady Sinclair and my sisters were here. They were tolerably well spent; in some of them I was enabled to return to the evening service. Our good pastor was absent last Lord's-day, having lost a sister, who died in the Lord. To-day Mr Stewart gave us a delightful sermon on Christ the Resurrection and the Life. It came home to my heart. Surely I possess this spiritual life. I feel something within that lives to God, that delights in God, that cannot exist without God, that must be derived from God. And if this new nature be, in the first instance, imparted without a right or title, it shall be preserved and strengthened unto everlasting life. These and such thoughts have been very joyful to me this day. I also felt truly grateful to the Almighty that there is such a change to the better in my Gospel privileges here. Oh, thanks be unto God for this!

"*Dec. 15.* — We little know what a day may bring forth. Nearly a fortnight ago I fell down thirteen steps of a stair, and was much bruised; but, most providentially, had no bone broken, and was not otherwise injured. It is singular that this fall has been the means of prayer being answered : and, between a sense of gratitude for that, and for my merciful preservation, my heart has been full of thankfulness and praise. I was about a week confined to bed; but never was God so present with me in illness. I could pray always, and rejoice too. Mr Stewart visits me often, and has been a great comfort

to me. I was still unable to go out to-day. My dear
daughter and Mr Reade, with his little boy, are now here.

"*Jan. 5*, 1845. — I am now able to attend in God's
house, and have been there the two last Sabbaths. I am
happy with many of my family about me; but, alas!
intercourse with others has in some measure deadened
my heart to God. I look back to my sick-bed with
something like regret, for then I was with Him all day;
yet He will never leave nor forsake me.

"*March 20.* — How uncertain are all things here!
This day week Lady Sinclair, my kind friend and step-
mother, was taken ill with a bilious attack, and to-day
is in that state we cannot say when she may be taken
hence. I went in a chair to see her yesterday and to-day,
being unwell myself. It is a sorrowing family. I prayed
with them, and said what I could. Oh! for a sanctified
use of the afflictions that are thickening around them;
for my sister, Mrs Stewart, has long been also in a very
precarious way, but seems to rest on the Rock of Ages.
Lord, how soon may such a time as this come to me!
I feel this evening united to Christ.

"*27.* — How much have I to write this evening! My
kind friend, Lady Sinclair, is no more; my sister, Mrs
Stewart, also gone. I was much with the former; but her
recollection was greatly impaired, and she could say little
on any subject. I saw her after death. Ah! how solemn
was the scene! — how sad the feelings of her sorrowing
family. Yesterday she was consigned to the same grave
at Holyrood, where my father lies. Mrs Stewart gave
pleasing evidence of being in a state of salvation. Oh,
to be ready when my summons shall come! To-day I
commemorated my Lord's death in St. Luke's.

"*Rossdhu, Oct. 19.* — I think grace grows; but it is
downward growth. It is a greater sense of need, and a

feeling that none but Christ can help. To-day I was thinking that I have every reason to trust that 'the Beloved is mine', because He has made me so heartily willing to be saved in His own way.

"*Jan. 4*, 1846. — I begin another year in health and comfort. This is the first day of the Concert for Prayer. I heartily joined in petitioning for an abundant outpouring of the precious Spirit; and I intend meeting with the servants during the week, in accordance with the appointment of our Church. I had an answer to prayer last week. How merciful is our God!

"*25.* — Probably the last Sabbath here, as we propose leaving for Edinburgh on Wednesday. I pray earnestly for a blessing on the congregation and its pastor, and on the parish — a new minister having been appointed for the Established Church. I do hope that this change will not prove unimportant, but that some good may come of it, and the hand of God be seen in it. I put my trust in Him for many things now depending on His providence.

"*18, Ainslie-place, Edinburgh, April 12.* — Since writing here a fortnight ago, I have gone through a good deal. A few days after, I became very feverish, and about a week was nearly confined to bed. I suffered also, and still suffer, from a depressing nervousness, which is hard to bear — disturbing my rest at night, and taking away my peace by day. Yet I think this illness has been blessed to me. Christ has appeared very precious; and although at times I could scarcely see my interest in Him, at other times I could embrace the simple promise, and hold Him fast, and not let Him go without a blessing. Sick and in bed last Lord's-day, I could do nothing but offer a few words of prayer. To-day I am able to be up, and am rapidly recovering; but being nervous, I thought, 'How shall I spend my sacred hours?' Looking through some books that had been lent me by my sister Catherine, I alighted on 'The True Christian', by Jones, of Creaton. Here I found much just suited to my need. All seemed encouraging; and many times to-day I have been receiving Christ and all His fulness. In writing of this illness, I must not forget to notice my many temporal blessings. God has given me all I possibly could desire. Truly, 'He has made all my bed in my sickness'.

"*19*. — Although still feeble, I have been progressing towards complete recovery during the week. Thanks to a gracious God! I have felt great benefit from this illness. I never so strongly saw my need of Christ, nor so fully closed with Him. Reading this morning in Jones's little book, I felt assured that what he describes as certain marks of the new nature — the love of God for what He is; the love of holiness; the love of the Spirit wherever seen; the love of the law — I felt convinced that these marks are mine, and something like assurance grew upon it.

"*26*. — I communicated in Free St. Stephen's, and scarcely ever enjoyed so much in the sacramental feast. I was fed in last week's preparatory services; but especially to-day, both in the sanctuary and at home, God was present. I awoke early, and, before rising, read with much delight the sixth chapter of John. Mr Gillies, on the love of Christ, from John xiii. 1, was truly delightful. Dr James Buchanan served the second table, and followed in the same strain, from 'Christ loved the Church, and gave Himself for it'. I have heard soul-refreshing truths, and I have given myself to the Lord, and rejoice in His love. God enabling me, I will henceforth confide in Him more.

"*Rossdhu, June 28*. — Many weeks have elapsed since I was able to note down my spiritual state and feelings.

I have been very ill; and after coming here from Edinburgh, was obliged to return to it for medical advice. The Almighty directed me to Dr Simpson, who at once saw the root of the evil, and whose method of treatment has, under Providence, given me great relief. The nervousness which so distressed me is gone. I have had a sight of death; for when one attack followed another, I often thought I might not recover. Alas! I never can view it with that desire to depart which many of God's children feel. However, in this, as in everything else, I must lean upon the Beloved, and hope He will guide me in safety through the dark valley. I seem to have been at school, and trust I have learned something, especially my helplessness, worthlessness, utter insufficiency. Against this could I but set Christ's strength, worth, sufficiency, all would be well. I was five weeks in Edinburgh, and returned two days ago. God has mercifully kept my little grandson in health during my absence, and all has been mercifully ordered.

"*July 5.* — Not well, but continuing to recover. Was at church, and heard a missionary, Mr Strachan, preach, on Luke i. 77-79. How dark, how awful would have been our thoughts regarding futurity, had not the tender mercy of our God caused the Day-spring to visit us, giving knowledge of salvation and the remission of sins! Blessed knowledge! most needful remission. Deeply, most deeply do I feel my need of it."

With the following letter to the Rev. Mr Macdonald, of Plockton, we conclude this chapter. This faithful minister was endeavouring to carry through some young men in their education as Gaelic preachers, an object to which Lady Colquhoun often and cheerfully contributed.

"*Rossdhu, Sept. 24*, 1846.

"Dear Mr Macdonald,— I received your kind letter this morning, and you see I lose no time in replying. I have indeed been a great invalid, at least I thought myself so. No doubt, many of God's dear children suffer much more, and I had every comfort to alleviate. He 'made all my bed in my sickness'. I am now, through mercy, very much better. Oh! it was sweet to me, when little able to pray for myself, to hope that some of God's people prayed for me. I was ashamed when I read in your letter that thrice a day you remembered me! Dear Sir, I can only say I value it more than tongue can tell. I often pray that any blessing asked for me may be largely given to those who ask themselves. You rightly judge that I have been longing for the sanctified use of affliction, more, I hope, than for its removal. It has laid me very low, and this is the greatest benefit I can perceive. I felt, and do feel, such a poor creature, weak, helpless, inconsistent, and sinful, that, were it not for the freeness of grace, I could have no hope. Yet, 'the foundation standeth sure'. Blessed, precious truth! On the promises I hang, and I ask and wish for nothing but what God has promised to give. And 'is He a man that He should lie? or the son of man that He should repent?'

"I did not know you had been laboring in Skye. I should like to hear your opinion of the awakening there. You are sent, I have no doubt, where there is work for you, although possibly you may not see it. One prescription of my medical adviser I do not feel palatable — that I must spend next winter, if spared, in England. But it is the Lord who sends me there. 'As Thou wilt', I desire to say. Oh! I felt touched by your observation, that I shall be here whilst God has any work to do *with* me or *in* me; and what would faith desire more? Ah, it

is the want of faith that would lead us to wish to remain
in this cold, comfortless world. Pray, dear Mr M., that in
me it may be strengthened, and that the Spirit — that
best, that promised, that purchased gift may be given me
in all its fulness, to enlighten and sanctify.

"I propose remaining at Rossdhu till November, when
I intend to remove to the south of England; but it is not
yet fixed where. Like Abraham, 'I go out not knowing
whither I go'. I inclose 10*l.* for your young men, who,
I am happy to learn, continue promising. May God grant
you and your hearers all needful supplies of grace! May
He be your sun and shield wherever you are!

"I remain, yours in the best of bonds,

" JANET COLQUHOUN."

CHAPTER VII

Precious in the sight of the Lord is the death of his saints.

— Psalm cxvi. 15.

The quiet chamber where the Christian sleeps,
And where, from year to year, he prays and weeps;
Whence, in the midnight watch, his thoughts arise
To those bright mansions where his treasure lies,—
How near it is to all his faith can see !
Yes, for that bliss unspeakable, unseen,
Is ready, and the veil of flesh between
A gentle sigh may rend, and then display
The broad, full splendour of an endless day.

Jane Taylor.

THE last chapter left the subject of this Memoir in shattered health; and from its depressing influence on the nervous system, the illness of that spring was at first peculiarly painful. The temperament of Lady Colquhoun was in unison with her sober judgment, and any deviations from its habitual tranquility were generally in a cheerful direction; and so seldom was her religious experience tinctured with gloom, that she had a very imperfect sympathy with the deep dejection of some eminent Christians, in whose biography she otherwise found delight and instruction. When, therefore, dreary or disconsolate weeks were appointed, she felt as if some strange thing had happened to her; but, instead of yielding to despondency, her sound understanding ascribed to its real pathological origin this withdrawment of sensible comfort, and with unshaken confidence she rested still on the Rock of her Salvation; and through her heavenly Father's tender mercy, this trying attendant on her malady was ere long succeeded by her wonted serenity.

Having come to Rossdhu in May, as has already been mentioned, she was obliged to return to Edinburgh for medical advice almost immediately. There, in much weakness, she spent the month of June; and we have now before us the notes, neatly, but feebly written, in which she conveyed tidings of her progress to her servants at home. To her attached housekeeper she wrote —

"*Monday*. — Your few lines, which I received this morning, gave me pleasure — to hear of the dear child's keeping well, and that all is going on comfortably. I am able to be up now, and in the parlor; but this last illness has thrown me back. I would say I am sorry, but am silenced by the thought — it is the Lord. Dr Simpson is now to go on with his prescriptions, to which the Lord *can* give efficacy if so seemeth Him good. But what if now should be His time to call me hence? I should be 'also ready'. He will do well. I do not know that there is much cause for alarm. I have less nervousness, and sleep better. We have comfortable lodgings. I am in good hands. (Deut. xxxiii. 3.) I am happy you had such good assistance at the communion.

"Your sincere friend,— J. C."

To her little grandson, now two years old, she had always shown the tenderest affection, and a chief part of her present trial was separation from him. Many of these notes are addressed to his nurse :—

"*May 20*. — I was very glad indeed to hear that my dear little boy continued strong, and was behaving well.

May God in mercy watch over him, and bring me back
to him in comfort! I sometimes feel the thought that
(poor little fellow!) he cannot understand why I have left
him. I am going on with the means prescribed, and have
less of the nervousness than I had, and I sleep better. I
am out as much as possible, and have every reason to be
thankful for goodness and mercy following me."

In the beginning of July she returned to Dumbartonshire, recruited; but on the 18th of that month an aguish
fever compelled her to hasten back to Edinburgh. There
again the means were blessed; and she recovered strength
enough to hear Dr Gordon and Mr Gillies preach, and
was able to pay a visit to the venerable widow of her
old pastor, Dr Buchanan. When Lady Colquhoun rose
to take leave, her aged friend insisted on accompanying
her to the door; and to the gentle remonstrance of her
neice, replied, "It is the last time." She did not think
that the younger was to go first, for her "own time was
not yet".

From Edinburgh, about the middle of August, she
proceeded to Helensburgh, and was sufficiently well to
take a lively interest in every movement affecting the
welfare of the Redeemer's kingdom. She had there, in
the preceding year, organized a branch of the Irish Home
Mission; and whilst its affairs gave her some occupation,
she was greatly cheered by accounts of the progress made
by Hindoo girls attending the schools of her favorite
Society in India. A month's sojourn on the coast
apparently revived her strength; and at the period of
her final return to Rossdhu, her habitual language was
gratitude to the Father of mercies. Peaceful slumber was
a boon which she now frequently enjoyed, and had learned
exceedingly to prize; and in the mornings she would
frequently say, "How thankful should I be when I think

of Mrs Cathcart!" Mrs C. had been deprived of rest at
night for a long time before her death — the only true
repose she could obtain being a short sleep in the evening,
on a sofa in the drawing-room.

On the 29th of September, when out walking, she was
overtaken in a shower, and obliged to seek shelter under
a tree. She herself apprehended no injury, and smiled
at the excessive caution of her family in sending out
cloaks and shawls. Next morning, however, she complained of sore-throat and fever; and although that
morning she appeared at the breakfast-table, and for two
days continued to go about and converse with her usual
cheerfulness, she evidently grew worse, and before Sabbath the 4th of October, she had taken to that bed from
which she was never again to arise. On that first Sabbath
of her illness, one of the servants, to whom she had often
spoken on the concerns of her soul, came into the room;
and, after saying a few kind words to her, Lady Colquhoun offered to pray with her, as she had frequently
done in other days. The brief but touching prayer will
not readily be forgotten by her on whose behalf it was
offered, all the rather, that every utterance had now become an exertion. To one of her family that day she
said emphatically, " 'Christ is all my salvation and all my
desire.' I hope for salvation in nothing but Christ."

At an early period of her illness she sent for Sir James,
desiring to speak to him alone. She told him that before
she became too ill, she wanted to give directions about her
funeral; that she did not wish to have any one invited
but the nearest relations, and that it should be quite
private. She then sent for her youngest son, and with
perfect composure told them her apprehension as to the
result, adding, "I die at the foot of the cross." Next day
she gave her youngest son directions regarding certain

charities, one of which was, that the sum she had paid
for the education of a theological student should be
continued till his college course was ended. "I see," she
said, "that you are affected; but I know that you will
pay attention to my wishes, as I have not left them as
bequests in my will." She then subjoined with great
earnestness, "Christ is my Portion; and, oh! what a
Portion! Seek that Portion."

A message had been sent to Edinburgh for Dr Simpson.
His partner, Dr Keith, arrived on the 6th, and stayed all
night; Dr Simpson came on the 9th; and during the remainder of her illness — an attack of dysentery, then
prevalent — one or other of these distinguished prac-
titioners was frequently with her, doing all that skill and
kindness could devise, often to the great temporary relief
of their patient. But from her first seizure she herself
seemed to have only one impression regarding the issue.
About a week after its commencement she said to one
of the household, "Mrs L., I am convinced that this
illness is to end in death; and I have just one hope —
only one — and that is, the finished work of Jesus." On
her attendant expressing a hope that she might recover,
she answered, "Oh, no! And for me to live would be
Christ, but to die will be gain — unspeakable gain";
and then, after a short prayer, she musingly added, "And
shall I see Him as He is — so soon? And shall I join
the redeemed around the throne? Overwhelming thought!"
The next day — and it was the only day that she so
complained — she spoke as if under a cloud, and
requested that those words might be read to her (Isa.
xliii. 1-3), "Fear not : for I have redeemed thee, I have
called thee by thy name; thou art mine. When thou
passest through the waters, I will be with thee; and
through the rivers, they shall not overflow thee : when

thou walkest through the fire, thou shalt not be burned; neither shall the flame kindle upon thee. For I am the Lord thy God, the Holy One of Israel, thy Saviour." But after that she seemed to be no more disturbed, often saying, "What a blessing it is that the enemy is kept away!" And from her lips were constantly dropping such expressions as, "The righteous hath hope in his death." "I know that my Redeemer liveth." "I cannot praise Him as I would; but I shall yet praise Him in perfection; yes, through all eternity."

She earnestly desired to see her daughter, Mrs Page Reade; but as the distance was great, feared that she might not reach Rossdhu in time to see her alive.

It was a great delight to her when her second son arrived from Edinburgh. She took his hand, saying, "That dear hand!" and after conversing cheerfully and minutely with him about his family, she ended by affectionately giving him her blessing.

Two lovely features of Christian character were very observable during this illness, a sweet acquiescence in the will of God and a constant mindfulness of others. Her sufferings were often very great, but she bore them without a murmur. On one occasion when the pain was violent, and in eagerness for speedy relief many palliatives were tried in quick succession, she said to one of the servants, "I fear you will think me impatient"; and the servant, who was only thinking of her mistress's sufferings, could give no answer but by bursting into tears. Another time, when her daughter was expressing the hope that she might yet be spared to them, her answer was, "And would you wish to keep me here? You don't know what I suffer." Then recollecting how these words might be understood, and alarmed at the idea of their conveying an impression of repining, with a look of anguish she exclaimed, "Oh, do I complain? I did not mean to complain. I *retract* these words." And when there was any abatement of suffering, she took care to apprize those near her, often by a single word when she could say no more, "Better, easy — easier," or "The Lord be praised for that." And in perfect self-forgetfulness, her great concern was for the health and comfort of those who ministered to her. In deep weakness she would remember the minutest precautions lest her daughter might catch cold sitting by her bedside over-night. During her own sickness the oldest inmate of the establishment was very low — the aged nurse, Mrs Barbara Graham. For years this faithful servant had been very frail and almost bed-ridden, and now, like her kind mistress, she was rapidly sinking; and to Lady Colquhoun it was a frequent anxiety, lest in their attendance on herself poor Graham should feel lonely or be any way overlooked. Amongst other relatives then at Rossdhu was her sister-in-law, Miss Colquhoun; and, speaking to her, she remarked, "You must find this a dull house," and she charged her servants to do all they could for the comfort of the guests, so that they might not be too much reminded of her own indisposition.

She could now take scarcely any sustenance, and as it was with the outer, so it was with the inner man. Her soul desired no dainty meat. And though she had many favorites in Christian authorship, during these latter days she never asked a portion from one of them. In the same way, though her memory was richly stored with hymns and spiritual songs, it looked as if the familiar stanzas were now forgotten. To her the Word of God was by this time everything. Such texts as Isaiah xxxii. 2, John xiv. 27, and xvii. 24, Romans viii. 32-39, were cordials which her spirit drank in when it cared for nothing else.

That passage in the Romans was the last to which she listened, and it is interesting to know that it is the last which was read to her beloved sister, Hannah. And though it was an effort to speak much, it seemed to make the effort less if it were some "tried word" that she was quoting. Just previous to this illness her daughter had been suffering from headache, and one day to her affectionate inquiry Miss Colquhoun replying that she was quite well, she rejoined, "He stayeth his rough wind in the day of his east wind." And at the time when her precarious state was first revealed to her family, perceiving Miss C. in deep distress, she gently said, " 'All his saints are in thy hand.' Do you remember that?" — alluding to a sermon preached in the foregoing spring, by Mr Gillies, the notes of which had afforded her singular delight. And at another time, turning to her daughter with a look of ineffable fondness, she repeated, "I will never leave thee no forsake thee."

About seven days before her departure she sent for all the servants, and spoke to them separately on the things of their eternal peace. To one she said, "Mary, you will soon lose me. Your day may not be so near, but it is coming; see that you have an interest in Christ before that; for what would I do to-day without Him? Mary, don't forget me, and remember all I have told you; and be sure you attend to the preaching of the Word. I benefited much from that in my own youth. And thank you for all that you have done for me." To another she said, "Look at me, a poor helpless creature, and don't put off preparing for eternity till you come to a death-bed. May the Lord be with you!" To another, "Now, I., be kind to Graham as long as you have her; but above all, oh remember your own soul! Good by, God bless you!" And to one in whose spiritual welfare she had much

interested herself, "Well, Mary, I wish to bid you good
by; for I will soon be taken from you. Never forget what
I have said to you; and oh, take Jesus for your friend,
and then there will be no fear of you; good by, Mary."
And great as was the exertion to her wasted frame, so
intent was she on addressing a word of kindness and
parting counsel to every one of them, that, having missed
one of the men-servants, she sent a messenger to bring
him. She had something suitable for each, and no one
was overlooked.

What else transpired within the precincts of that
hallowed chamber must be told in the words of filial
affection :— "She now felt as if her work were done. At
the same time she declared that she renounced all dependance on anything she had ever performed, as her best
was altogether sinful; adding, 'Christ is my hope, should
be my motto; I rely entirely on His finished work.' To
myself she said, 'My death will do more good than my
life could do; for it will show you more forcibly than
anything that can happen, the vanity of earthly things.'
After expressing in strong terms how much she felt at
leaving me behind, she said, 'I wish I could take you
with me; but God can make up my loss to you.' I told
her that a letter had come to her from her beloved friend,
Miss S. She said, 'Poor A.! little does she think of the
news that awaits her'; but she did not ask to have the
letter read. Indeed she was too ill to listen.

"Six days before her death, the nurse brought her
little grandson to the door of her chamber, and I asked
if she might bring him in. 'Oh, yes,' she replied, 'tell
her to bring him in that I may see him for the last time.'
Her eyes were now almost constantly closed, but she
raised them and looked on him with inexpressible tenderness. Then giving him her blessing, she prayed 'that the

Lord might make him a child of grace, and that, if spared, he might yet witness for His own cause.' She then said, 'I have given him up to God, and commit him to His care'; and gave his nurse her blessing. The dear child's look of infantine delight at again beholding his grand-mamma was touchingly contrasted with all besides in that solemn scene. She spoke of her daughter, Mrs Reade, and of the probability that she and Mr Reade were then on their way. 'But tell Helen how much I love her, and give my love to Mr Reade, and their dear, dear little boy.' That evening, when all the family who were then at home were assembled in her apartment, she desired a light to be brought near, and asked if they saw much change in her appearance; but though very wasted, it was wonder-ful how little alteration had come over that placid countenance.

"On the morning of the 17th, her sister and sister-in-law being about to leave, came to bid her farewell. To Miss Diana Sinclair she said, 'Set the Lord Jesus always before you, and it will be your comfort on your death-bed, as it is at this moment mine.' In a previous interview her sister had been much affected by her asking, 'Do I not remind you of Hannah?' When Miss Colquhoun after-wards came into the room, she likewise exhorted her to go to the Saviour, and embraced her affectionately and gave her her blessing. By that day's post intelligence was received that Mr and Mrs Reade would reach Rossdhu in the evening. They accordingly arrived at seven o'clock, having travelled day and night. The meet-ing, though affecting, was an inexpressible comfort to mother and daughter.

"On first seeing Mrs Reade, she repeated, 'I am so thank-ful, I am so thankful'; adding, 'Yesterday I never expected to see you again in this world; but how merciful is my gracious Lord to hear my prayers, that you may receive my parting blessing still!' And then she continued, 'But I am better to-day; indeed, I feel much better since you arrived; although you must find me much changed. However, we must look from this to the glorious change.' She then asked to see Mr Reade, and her young grandson, James Reade, for whom she had always evinced a great affection. He was then seven years old. She reminded him of the times when she used to take such pleasure in teaching him chapters from the Bible, and hymns, and when she used to tell him of Jesus' love to little children. She then asked him to repeat the last six verses of the eleventh chapter of Matthew, and then told him that she had no fears of death because she had cast her 'heavy load' on Jesus, who was willing to receive 'all' who 'came' to Him. And when she ended with saying, 'I trust, dear boy, we shall one day meet in heaven; there is plenty of room there,' and more to the same purport, tears filled the eyes of all who overheard her simple exhortation."

Being so much better that day, Mrs Reade asked what would be her own wishes in regard to recovery. She answered that her only tie to life now would be to be with them all, and then she said, "Perhaps it would be better if I went now, having advanced so far on the way; for even if I do recover from this illness, I shall sooner or later have to go through the same scene again, and at my period of life the time must be short."

"A few days before her death," — we resume Miss Colquhoun's narrative — "on being raised up, she remarked, with apparent satisfaction, that she could not see out of the window nor distinguish objects at any distance. Thankfulness was still a prominent trait of her disposition, and every relief from pain called forth some grateful acknowledgment. 'Thanks, Lord,' was her usual

emphatic expression every time she received her medicines
or such slight nourishment as she was able to take. Dr
Simpson's last visit was on the night of the 19th, and he
was again the means of alleviating her sufferings for a
time. He could do no more. She gradually relapsed, and
it was plain that her release could not be distant. She
herself seemed to long for it, and frequently repeated,
'Come, Lord Jesus, come quickly.' She asked if the
doctors would not know by her pulse how long she was
likely to last, and said to Mrs Reade, when they were
together alone, 'Now think if there is anything else you
would like to say or to ask; for my time is very short.'
Mrs R. replied, 'You seem very anxious to be gone.'
'Yes,' was the answer, 'the sooner the better now, for me
and for you too; but I must be patient.' She then said,
'Dearest H., you will never forget all I have said to you.
I sometimes fear I have not said enough to you all; but
I commit you to the Saviour.' Mrs R. said, 'I am sure it
rests with ourselves if we have not benefited as we ought.'
She replied, 'That's gratifying' — and after a few more
remarks, ended at that time by embracing her affectionately, and with great earnestness and solemnity gave her
the final blessing. She then desired Mrs R. to bring her
little boy, James Reade, that he might also receive her
parting blessing, and she took leave of him in a most
affectionate manner. On the evening of the 20th she
took an affectionate leave of her eldest and youngest
sons. She thanked my eldest brother for all his kindness
to her, particularizing some of her obligations to him,
and then she gave each of them her last blessing, adding,
'I hope to meet you all at the right hand of the Judge.'
After midnight she desired that I should endeavour to
procure some rest, and as her attendants promised to
come for me if Lady Colquhoun became worse, I com-

LIFE OF LADY COLQUHOUN 199

plied, the more readily as the violence of her sufferings
had now considerably abated. Towards morning she
showed her usual consideration for those around her. A
maidservant had sat up to relieve one of her regular
attendants; and when she was leaving the room, though
articulation was now very difficult, she said, 'Remember,
M., you must not go to your work as usual to-day.' That
morning, the 21st, I found her quiet, and apparently free
from pain, though evidently going home. Her eyes were
closed, but she was not asleep; for when I spoke she
threw her arms round my neck and kissed me affectionately. It was a mother's last embrace. She then said to
me, 'My Sarah, I have not given you my blessing. I pray
that God may bless you with all spiritual blessings in
heavenly places in Christ Jesus.' By and by she said, 'I
wish none to be with me but my family.' My sister and
I knew that this was in allusion to her last moments.
She again asked to see her little grandson, James Reade;
but when he was brought the shades of death had
obscured her sight. She said, 'Where is he? I cannot see
him.' Mrs R. put his hand within hers, and she grasped
it firmly, her lips moving as if in prayer. Mrs R. and I
sat down by her bed-side, and after a short interval I said
to her, 'We shall meet in heaven.' She returned no answer,
nor could I be sure that she heard me. I then said, 'And
Jesus is with you now.' She turned her head round to
me, and made an effort to reply, and by the expression
of her countenance I am quite certain that she understood
me. She spoke no more, and seemed as if in a soft sleep.
She faintly acquiesced when Mrs Reade asked if she
would like to see Mr Stewart, in whose visits she had
taken peculiar pleasure. She was quite unable to speak
to him when he arrived, but assented when asked if he
should pray. We kneeled down, and in a most solemn

and impressive prayer Mr S. commended her soul to God. After this she lingered, as if in a peaceful slumber, until three o'clock in the afternoon, when, without a struggle, a groan, or sigh, her willing spirit took its flight to those glorious realms for which she had longed so ardently. But so gentle, so imperceptible was her release, that for some time we could scarcely believe she was really gone. 'She was not, for God took her'; and after death her countenance retained the peaceful, tranquil look it had worn when living."

It was on Wednesday, October 21, 1846, that her shining path thus merged in perfect day. And on the following Saturday another pilgrimage ended. Mrs Graham only outlived by three days that kind and grateful mistress who had provided with every comfort her years of infirmity and decay. On Tuesday the 27th the chapel, which ten years before had received the remains of her husband, opened for the coffin of Lady Colquhoun. In compliance with her own request, she still wore her wedding-ring and a mourning-ring containing Sir James's hair. The funeral was private, but a few of the people in the neighbourhood sought and received permission to be present. Mr N. Stewart conducted the usual service before the precious remains were carried forth to the place of sepulture. It was exactly four weeks that day when last she looked on the tints of autumn. The copses were russet then, and the noble trees around the mansion wore their final drapery of scarlet, and brown, and gold, a sight which she used wonderfully to admire. But by the time the withered leaves were drifting into her grave, she needed not to mind that it was winter in the earth; for, instead of the roughening lake and the searing forest, God had showed her "the pure river, clear as crystal", and "the tree of life, yielding fruit every month", and whose leaves "heal the nations": and, better still, she had found her life-long wish; she "served God and saw His face".

On the following Sabbath her funeral sermon was preached from Heb. vi. 12, in the Free Church of Luss, by her much-valued friend and minister, the Rev. Neil Stewart; and in the parish church an appropriate and impressive sermon was delivered from John xiv. 27, by the Rev. Robert Wright. And when the various religious societies and charitable institutions with which she had been connected held their next meetings, they placed on record their fervent tributes of affection and esteem.*

---

* In the "Thirty-sixth Annual Report of the Gaelic School Society", appeared the following just and discriminating notice, which we have much satisfaction in transferring to these pages:—

"Before passing from what refers to the Ladies' Association, your Committee lament to say, that in common with all the friends of religion in this land, they have, in the death of Lady Colquhoun, to mourn over the removal from among them of one who formed a distinguished member of Christ's Church upon earth — one who adorned the profession of Christianity, and who formed an invaluable friend of the Gaelic School Society, as Treasurer of the Ladies' Association, and one of the Society's Vice-Patronesses. The Committee have a melancholy satisfaction in transferring to these pages the minute which they have recorded elsewhere, on this affecting event in the history of the past year — with the sentiments expressed in which, they feel assured, all the friends of the Society will heartily sympathize:—

" 'It is with deep concern and solemnity of feeling that the Committee have now to record the death of Lady Colquhoun of Luss, who for several years has acted as Treasurer to the Ladies' Auxiliary Association in connexion with this Society. They are deeply sensible that the event is felt by the religious world to be a public loss. The influence of Lady Colquhoun's holy and consistent life; the character of her writings, uniting spirituality of tone, and faithfulness in sentiment, with mental acuteness and elegance of diction; the munificence of her offerings to the cause of Christ, which was ever dear to her; and, above all, the efficacy of her fervent prayers, combined to render her at once the ornament of her numerous circle of friends, and an esteemed and truly valuable member of the Church of Christ. The removal of one who, in the providence and by the grace of God, occupied such a position, especially at such a time, is an occurrence which

Tall and dignified, with an ample and intellectual fore-
head, and with beautiful Grecian features, lighted up by
a fine complexion and an eye mildly penetrating, there
was something peculiarly prepossessing in the youthful
appearance of Lady Colquhoun. A total absence of

cannot fail solemnly to affect the minds of all who are concerned
for the cause of truth.

"'But the Committee feel that their province is specially to
regard this event in its bearing on the Gaelic School Society. It
is with melancholy interest they record the lively and affectionate
concern uniformly evinced by Lady Colquhoun for the prosperity
of this Institution. In its times of difficulty and trial she was its
faithful, zealous, self-denying, devoted friend. When it pleased
the Lord to vouchsafe to its efforts any marked tokens of His
countenance and blessing, such tidings were ever to her the
occasion of humble gratitude and praise. The Society received
largely of her bounty, and no doubt was often the subject of her
prayers. Reflecting on the high place which she was enabled to
occupy, the Committee feel that in her removal by the hand of
Providence, one of their chief earthly props has been taken away.

"'But it is the Lord's hand which has smitten. He is teaching
by this event to "cease from man", and to look with undivided
reliance to His grace and power. He will graciously maintain His
own cause, and command the light to shine even out of darkness.
The Committee would, therefore, while feeling the stroke, desire
to go on with their humble labors, encouraging themselves in the
Lord. In the meantime, they would take comfort in reflecting on
the well-grounded hope which they are warranted to cherish
regarding their valued and lamented friend. And while they pray
that this solemn event may be sanctified to themselves and to all
who knew the Christian worth and zeal of Lady Colquhoun, they
fervently trust that the Lord will be pleased specially to bless it
to her sorrowing family and relatives. To them the bereavement
is, humanly speaking, irreparable. But their sorrow may well be
turned into joy, for it is written, "Blessed are the dead which die
in the Lord, from henceforth; yea, saith the Spirit, that they may
rest from their labours; and their works do follow them."'"

The same event was thus noticed in the Report on Female
Education in India :—

"During the past year, not a few of those who once were
distinguished associates with us in this great enterprise, whose
tenderest sympathies were long ago aroused for the manifold
sorrows of the daughters of India, and whose delight it was to
devise and to prosecute plans which should ensure their complete
and final redemption from all their woes, have ceased to be
engaged in such occupations on earth. Lady Colquhoun, of Luss,
one of your Society's earliest and most highly-valued friends,

affectation superadded the perfecting charm of a sweet
unconsciousness. Her elevated mind and graceful manners
were instinct with feminine refinement and inherent
nobility; and though in later years her complexion had
faded and her figure stooped, there came the more

with whose enlightened Christian counsels and prevailing intercessions it was for long so eminently favored; and Major John
St. Clair Jameson, of Bombay, whose honoured name is associated
in the minds of so many in this country, with their first feelings
of commiseration for the fate of their afflicted sisters in the East,
as well as other less distinguished, but not less devoted friends of
the cause, have within the last few months rested from their
labors and entered upon their reward.

"Regarding the elevated character of the late lamented Patroness (Lady Colquhoun), the Committee feel that it would be
superfluous now to remark. The distinguished gifts she possessed,
which all were consecrated to the noblest and best of purposes;
her matured graces, which served so eminently to adorn the
doctrine of her God and Saviour — these were well known and
appreciated in the Churches while she was yet here, and will
long be cherished in the fond remembrance of many, now that
she is gone. But the Committee are assured that the following
brief extract from the last letter written to your agent at Calcutta
by their revered departed friend, indicating, as it does, the views
and feelings she entertained regarding India during her last days
on earth, will be regarded as possessing peculiar interest by all
the members of the Society :—

" 'I would wish to encourage the hope that there is a blessing
in store for India. The windows of heaven seem opening; put in
your claim for a share of the refreshing shower. Hope on! Wait
on! Urge and work on! After toil, rest is sweet; and the rest
that remains for the people of God will be most welcome to
those who have borne the burden and heat of the day.' "

To which must be added an extract from the Sixth Address of
the Ladies' Society in Scotland in Aid of the Home Mission of
the Presbyterian Church in Ireland :—

"We cannot close this Report without alluding to the loss
which our Society has sustained in the removal, by death, of its
much-respected Patroness, Lady Colquhoun. To her this Society
chiefly owned its origin. In her death, the cause of the Home
Mission may be said to have lost, in Scotland, its oldest and
most influential friend. Besides defraying the College expenses
of one of the converts now training for the ministry (Mr Keegan),
she ever contributed readily with her means to the numerous
demands of the Mission in other ways. The want of her generous
support and Christian counsel in the management of this Society
will be long and deeply felt," &c., &c.

brightly forth the reassuring gentleness, the delicate consideration, and the tact in diffusing happiness, which are among the loveliest attributes of the Christian lady.

The basis of her natural goodness was truth. Even before it was hallowed into "godly sincerity", her disposition was unusually open and candid; and after she had learned to live in the recollection — "Thou, God, seest me", she became studiously exact and scrupulous. It was not only that she forbade her servants to use the fashionable equivocation, "Not at home", but all her intercourse and correspondence were pervaded by a most rigid adherence to the rule of "Yea, yea, and Nay, nay". And this elaborate truthfulness re-acted on all her character. It materially promoted her self-knowledge, and contributed to her growth in grace. And the blessed consciousness that she had never wilfully flattered or maligned, enabled her to mingle in all society with a cheerful security and a goodwill as obvious as it was genuine. Nor was she "afraid of evil tidings. Her heart was fixed, trusting in the Lord."

The steps by which she was brought to the knowledge of the Saviour, have been traced in the foregoing pages; but, as a brief review of her religious experience, and as an expression of her matured feelings and sentiments very near the close of life, we are sure the reader will peruse with interest the following letter. It was addressed to a faithful minister in the Highlands, towards the erection of whose church she had previously contributed, and is dated Oct. 28, 1845 :—

"MY DEAR SIR, — I know not how to refuse the request made in your letter, which I received a short time since; and yet I am assured nothing but misconception on your part could have induced you to make it. I am to tell you

'my sentiments and feelings when Jehovah causes the
light of His face to shine on me.' Alas! alas! how rare is
this! And I am to say what are my 'views and feelings
when, in chastisement, His face is hid.' Here, also, I am
at fault; for I know little of the heights and depths to
which so many of God's people are subjected. I have been
led in green pastures, and beside the still waters. One
thing I have learned, and from the bottom of my heart
I feel it — my utter nothingness. But do not think my
speaking thus is the sign of deep humility. Ah! no. I am
sensible you will not think the worse of me for saying so.
I fear to write of myself — I cannot, without sin. I may
write, then, of my Saviour; *there* is a theme upon which
I need not dread to enlarge. And I can with truth say,
that each step in my journey through life leads me, with
more undivided confidence, to rest on Him alone, without
reference to anything else but His finished work.

> " 'Nothing in my hand I bring,
> Simply to thy cross I cling;
> Naked, come to thee for dress;
> Helpless, look to thee for grace;
> Foul, I to the Fountain fly;
> Wash me, Saviour! or I die.'

"I have been led very gradually and gently in the
divine life. I never knew the pangs of the new birth; and
at first had slight views of the depravity of the heart, or
of the need of salvation by Christ. These things were
more articles of my creed than the conviction of the soul.
I believed them chiefly because the Bible told me they
were true. But years have supervened, and proof that the
heart is deceitful above all things and desperately wicked
has not been awanting; and hence, if saved at all, I now
feel it must be by grace through faith. One thing I
believe, is rather singular in my experience — that I was

more induced to devote myself to God by the beauty of the Divine character, and the lovely precepts of the Gospel, than by any other consideration. And still, when I can get but a glimpse of these things in anything like their transcendant glory, my heart is fixed. But I dare not go on in this strain. I am much afraid you will think me very different from what I am. I have wandered from my subject. I was going to write of the Saviour. I think, then, the Apostle Peter is very happy in the expression when he calls Him 'precious'. What so precious as that which we cannot have a moment's peace without? What so precious as that in which perfection dwells — where beauty alone shines? Or, what is of equal value to us with the God-man, who saves us from everlasting perdition, and makes us 'partakers of *His holiness?*' These are commonplace and well-known truths; but we need to be reminded of them; and, ah! how slightly are they impressed upon the heart! Yet still — *still* we must say, however listlessly and feebly, *Christ is precious!* Many, I know, say it with more devout affections than I can do. But say so I must and will, as He Himself shall enable me. He must take my heart; I cannot give it Him. You, my dear Sir, have a high honor assigned to you in having the everlasting Gospel to preach. Let not your hands hang down; you have a noble cause, a good Master, and assurance, of some measure at least, of success. I believe ministers are often little aware of the effect of their preaching. I knew a man of God, now in his grave, or rather, I should say, now before the throne (Dr Buchanan, of the Canongate), who told me that he had just heard of one who had died in the Lord, and mentioned, on his death-bed, that Dr B.'s preaching had been the means of his conversion twenty years before; and all that time he was ignorant of the circumstance.

When very young, Dr B. was of great use to myself; but I dared not have told him so for long after. I have now, as far as I know it, and according to my ability, complied with your request. May not I, with equal reason, expect that a word from you will benefit me? But I do not wish to tax you. I know the many calls you must have upon your time, and I, too, have sometimes as much writing as I can well accomplish."

The pervading element in her piety was an adoring attachment to this Divine Redeemer. The desire to see His cause triumphant in the world impelled her efforts in the many Societies of which she was an assiduous member. Regard for His honor prompted all the more important actions of her later life. The hope of introducing others to His transforming friendship made her personally and with the pen, in books and in conversation, in cottage visits and in exalted society, "instant in season and out of season". And the belief that they belonged to the Saviour endeared to her obscure or imperfect Christians, just as the perception of earnestness in His service drew her regard towards ministers of ordinary gifts, and made her a docile or delighted listener to sermons which would have been reckoned common-place by hearers more fastidious or less fervent. And closely allied to this was her unusual confidence in prayer. It was one of the sisters at Bethany who said to Jesus, "Lord, if thou hadst been here, my brother had not died. But I know, that even now, whatsoever thou wilt ask of God, God will give it thee." And the subject of this record had a confidence in the Saviour's grace and power akin to that of Martha, and for a similar reason — she had a like affection. In everything, by prayer and supplication, she made known her requests; and her Diary abounds in notices of answered prayer.

"Ye are the light of the world." The believer fulfils his exalted function when, filled with the Divine Spirit, he so acts that in his graciousness men are reminded of the grace of God. "*Let* it shine," and "let it *so* shine that men may see your good works, and glorify your Father in heaven." The piety of Lady Colquhoun was spontaneous, effusive, evenly, like a lamp abundantly replenished; and its bright spirituality at once reminded the beholder of its heavenly Source. And we know not that we can better describe what manner of person she was in this respect, than by copying the words of her own minister, and those of her eldest brother.

"It has been my privilege," says the Rev. Neil Stewart, "to converse with not a few persons of Christian character; but I have not received the same pleasure or benefit from all. In conversing with some, I have felt my affections restrained, my spirits depressed, and a painful feeling of discontent predominating in my mind. But I never left Lady Colquhoun without feeling my affections purified, my heart warmed, and my spirit raised in humble thankfulness to God for His goodness, and in earnest desire to be conformed to His image, and to do all things to His glory. This, I am persuaded, was the result of the peculiar character of her piety, which was alike devoid of that asceticism which contracts the affections, and that enthusiasm which impairs the judgment. Like one of her favorite authors, John Howe, she dwelt with much delight on the character and attributes of God as revealed in the face of Jesus Christ, and by the habitual contemplation of them it seemed as if she were more and more conformed to the same image."

And to his niece, Sir George Sinclair writes :— "I look back with unfeigned satisfaction on all my personal intercourse with my beloved sister, because I am quite certain that we never exchanged a hasty word, and never harboured towards each other an unkind feeling, even for a single moment. Her piety was entirely free from moroseness or gloom. She was never highly elevated, and never unduly depressed. Though always dignified, her manner was often playful. She did not exact from others a strict and undeviating observance of the rules which she had laid down for her own guidance, and though uncompromising as to all principles of grave importance, she was always inclined to the side of lenity and indulgence when she differed from others in matters of minor moment. You are aware with what enthusiastic strength of zeal and conviction she espoused the interests of the Free Church; and yet she always discussed that very exciting question with me (who had reluctantly, but conscientiously, remained connected with the Established Church) in a spirit of charity and forbearance which is much more frequently enforced than exemplified. On the whole, I have never seen any character so blameless and harmless, and without rebuke; so free from infirmities, and so adorned by virtues. She lived much *with* her Saviour in prayer, which is the surest resource for being enabled to live *like* Him in daily conversation."

Thus devoted and thus endowed, it was her blessedness to accomplish much for that Redeemer whom she loved so ardently and followed so affectionately. In the nearest circle of her kindred, in her own household, amongst her younger and older neighbors, to the poor of other places, to casual visitors, she was the source of incalculable benefits. Irrespective of her munificent contributions and unwearying exertions in the cause of Christian philanthropy, the friends of the Gospel felt a perpetual solace in her presence, and were comforted to think that in the most polished society was exhibited such a specimen of pure and consistent piety. Her light shone to the last, and was brightest at the end; and her Father in heaven was glorified.

Like Hannah and Jessie Sinclair, we invite our younger readers to choose "that better part, which shall not be taken from them"; assuring them that, if at the foot of the Cross they lay down some things that are brilliant, they will there obtain in return all that is beautiful. When these happy sisters found the Saviour they did not lose their taste for intellectual enjoyments, nor their zeal for personal improvement; but they found a Friend all-wise and ever-present, who in scenes of anxiety kept them calm and self-possessed, and in the midst of flattery preserved them sober-minded; and who, along with the forgiveness of sin, imparted to their character a depth and a delicacy which cannot be derived from courtly rules or from culture the most assiduous. In their parallel history is seen how gracefully with feminine refinement may be combined homely duties and labors of practical beneficence; and it proclaims once more how essential to eminent piety are self-knowledge, watchfulness, and prayer. And surely, in the blessed confidence that through His interposition lives so lovely have been once more united, we have another reason for loving and adoring that Redeemer who has already transferred so much of earth to heaven.

> They have been brought with gladness great,
>   And mirth on ev'ry side,
> Into the palace of the King,
>   And there they shall abide.

FINIS